"I must die like a kernel of wheat that falls into the furrows of the earth. Unless I die, I will be alone, a single seed. But my death will produce many new wheat kernels—a plentiful harvest of new lives."

. . . . The Living Bible

Dedication

With gratitude and deep appreciation
I dedicate this book to:
My friend, Kitty (Catherine W. Dukehart)
who supported and encouraged my studies at
Emory University;
My mentor and advisor at Emory University,
the late Prof. Fred R. Crawford, who said,
"Don't write a thesis. Write a book;"
My family---Husband Jack,
for his patience and good humor;
Son John and his wife, Kathy;
Sons Bill and Bob, whose resilience
and zest for life have sustained me;
and, of course,
Mitch.

Acknowledgements

I am grateful to so many people. To name them all is impossible. To name a few is a privilege. I thank my extended family, my friends and colleagues who were and continue to be a part of my process of surviving, healing, and living.

I thank the staff and volunteers of The Link Counseling Center in Atlanta who lived through my healing day by day and who keep me honest and growing.

I thank friends and members of the support groups known as The Compassionate Friends and The Survivors of Suicide who shared their pain and sorrow, gave me hope, and taught me about survival.

I. B.

MY SON...
MY SON...

A Guide to Healing After A Suicide in the Family

by
IRIS BOLTON
with
Curtis Mitchell

Cover
by
Zelpha

COMMENT

Dr. Billy Graham says:

One of life's blackest moments comes with the realization that your dead child has rejected you, and slammed the door. Iris Bolton cites chapter and verse of her long struggle to escape from the tomb of her memories in order to emerge with enough strength to find a new life.

Jerome A. Motto M.D.
Professor of Psychiatry, University of California, says:

This book has a priceless message for every person who cares for others. If the reader has sustained a loss ... the message is one of realistic hope, of reassurance, of practical emotional support and healing. In the absence of loss, the message is one of such heightened awareness of what is of value in life that it generates the resolve to nurture those things which in turn can only reduce many of the painful aspects of life that are conducive to loss. Iris Bolton's message is courageous, forthright and to the point.

Copyright © 1983 Iris Bolton

All rights reserved. No part of this book may be reproduced by mimeograph, xerox, or any other method without permission in writing from the publisher, except by a reviewer who wishes to quote brief passages in connection with a review to be published in a newspaper or magazine, or by a writer-journalist or scholar who wishes to use excerpts in connection with an essay, article or a book on the same or kindred subjects. For information, address the Bolton Press, 1325 Belmore Way, NE., Atlanta, GA 30350, 404-393-1173.

Private first edition	December 1983
Private second edition	May 1984
Private third edition	September 1984
Private fourth edition	March 1985
Private fifth edition	September 1985
Private sixth edition	September 1986
Private seventh edition	March 1987
Private eighth edition	February 1988
Private ninth edition	August 1988
Private tenth edition	May 1989
Private eleventh edition	November 1989
Private twelfth edition	May 1991

CONTENTS

Part One: The Bitter Taste Of Hemlock

1. A Time to Fear — 1
2. Doomsday — 4
3. Formula for Survival — 9
4. A Promise I Can't Believe — 13
5. Healing Begins at Home — 18
6. The Magic of a Dream — 21
7. The Ups and Downs of Grief — 26
8. The Secret Anatomy of Depression — 29
9. Picking Up the Pieces — 36
10. The Miracle of Renewal — 39
11. The Making of a Survivor — 42
12. The Savage God Returns — 47
13. Another Kick in the Stomach — 51
14. You Can Make a Difference — 56

Part Two: Blueprint For Renewal

15. Sorrow Knows No Strangers — 60
16. A Time for Holding — 66
17. First Aid for Survivors — 70
18. Requiem for a Lost Lady — 74
19. My Son . . . My Son . . . — 80
20. Living, Loving, and Letting Go — 85
21. L'Envoi — 87

Appendices

Appendix A — 99
Appendix B — 102
Appendix C — 104
Appendix D — 107

Foreword

At bottom, life and death are our greatest teachers—if we shall but listen.

Iris Bolton's personal story of her son's suicide is a deeply moving, poignant one. It is a story of both a devastating tragedy and an exquisite triumph—and the agonizing, relentless, conflicted process connecting these two oppositional pulls.

We in our Western, ultra-scientific and technological society are just beginning to discover that death, from the beginnings of time, has always been present. Life and death are inextricably bound together in the process of living. All of us have known this all the time, but we have pretended that we didn't know what we knew. Until recently, we have chosen to keep death in the shadows and separated from the light of life. As a result, we have made ourselves more vulnerable to its pain and destruction. That this is true is well documented in this book.

I celebrate our growing consciousness that death is a Presence always present in all our lives. And living life in this manner of awareness gives us a new sense of personal power and freedom. We are better enabled to live, explore, experience, and know God's universe and Love as He intended—and thereby be more adequately prepared for the final journey . . . Home.

Iris Bolton's book is a powerful step in that direction.

                                                Leonard T. Maholick, MD
                                                Atlanta, Georgia
                                                August, 1983.

Preface

I don't know why.

I'll never know why.

I don't have to know why.

I don't like it.

I don't have to like it.

What I do have to do is make a choice
about my living.

What I do want to do is accept it and
go on living.

The choice is mine.

I can go on living, valuing every moment
in a way I never did before,
or I can be destroyed by it and,
in turn, destroy others.

I thought I was immortal.
That my family and my children were also.
That tragedy happened only to others.
But I know now that life is tenuous
and valuable.

So I am choosing to go on living,
making the most of the time I have,
valuing my family and friends
in a way never possible before.

Iris Bolton.

PART ONE:
THE BITTER TASTE OF HEMLOCK

1
A Time to Fear

Surviving the death of a dear one is to endure great pain. Surviving a *suicidal* death is to compound that pain with such embarrassments as public ridicule and private humiliation, and often exaggerated feelings of guilt and anger.

Fortunately, a ray of hope, indeed a new dawning, lies ahead because of what we are learning about grief. This hope is fueled by a new willingness to talk freely about death. The research of Dr. Elizabeth Kubler-Ross and others has led this understanding of healing.

We are also beginning to learn something about the causes of suicide, to discover assistance for the would-be suicide, and to help family and friends in the aftermath of suicide.

Most importantly, we are the beneficiaries of profound probings into thousands of aching minds and hearts by determined investigators who, at long last, have achieved an understanding of the mysterious emotional rhythms that control the healing of battered minds and tattered psyches.

Indeed, a new day awaits every victim who will dare to hope. Communion and love are available if such are needed. So are the steadying fruits of research and clinical experience. I can attest to their power, to the therapy they provide, and to their closing of stubborn wounds.

I can say this because I have been there.

I can say this because I became one of suicide's "walking wounded" on an unforgettable Saturday afternoon in February of 1977.

Why a person will take his own life has baffled a thousand generations. A modern survivor of such a personal and family tragedy is just as puzzled today as the survivor of 10,000 B.C. who lived in a cave.

Some of us are aware of recent investigations into this mystery by sociologists, statisticians, and psychologists. A few of us even know of that sub-specialty called suicidology. But the vast majority of us, almost totally uninformed of this issue, look on suicide with fear, with abhorrence, and with loathing. And all of us, regardless of intellect or knowledge, suffer deeply from guilt and grieving when it happens to us or our families.

We were an average family; upper-middle class, I suppose. My husband, Jack, was in the advertising business, owner of a successful agency that represented television and radio stations. Our four sons, ranging in age from 14 up to 22, were getting their education in various nearby schools and colleges, all except 20-year-old Mitch, who was the minstrel of the family. He had been trying to find himself in the world of music.

Typically of mothers whose kids are all in school, I had taken a job, first as a volunteer at The Link, a family counseling center, then nine years ago, as its director. Untypically, perhaps, we were also a kind of "public" family in that we loved music and sang and appeared a lot in public, even participating in several musicals for one good cause or another.

Early in his teens Mitch had demonstrated a rare talent for writing original songs and accompanying himself on guitar or piano. His interest at first was rock and roll, later jazz and blues. Sometimes he and I played guitars and sang together at schools, churches or hospitals.

But one should start at the beginning and nothing would please me more. But where oh where is the beginning of a death by one's own hand? When and where does the notion of self-destruction enter anyone's life? How does it walk on cat's-paws until it possesses one's soul? I have never found the answer nor has any other researcher in this bitter and arcane discipline. The truth is that there are many beginnings, perhaps as many as there are people, for each one of us is a universe in himself. Instead, I shall chart my own unpremeditated odyssey as clearly and honestly as I can. Perhaps even a single trail through the jungle that has grown up around the mystery of self destruction can help us toward the goal of survival.

2
Doomsday

What on earth is happening, I wondered.

My car rolled along our driveway to the carport where I saw several neighbors gathered about a truck that had backed up to our kitchen door. They seemed to be intent on loading something into its interior. Neither my husband nor my sons were visible. Something must have happened to our horse, I mused. A man left the group and hurried toward me. He was a close friend and neighbor. Norm's face was set now in a kind of crooked mask.

"What's going on?"

"Don't get out," he said. "We're going to the hospital."

"Who is it?"

"Mitch," he said.

"Motorcycle?" My son had become the owner of a motorcycle about which I had worried.

He said, "No, worse."

Although I was worried, I remembered that my trunk was full of spoilable groceries. "Wait, I have groceries in the trunk," I said.

As we drove to the hospital, I began to feel what I can only call the breath of death. I can't explain it, but it struck me like a cold draft, maybe like novocaine strikes an exposed nerve, and it paralyzed my tongue and blocked my hearing. If Norm and I spoke en route, I have no recollection of it. Emotions, I have since learned, can perform a lobotomy as efficiently as any brain surgeon's knife.

At the hospital, my husband, Jack, came to me across the broad sidewalk of the emergency entrance. Son John, my oldest, was at his shoulder. Their arms embraced me and someone said, "It's too late. He's gone."

"What happened?"

"He shot himself."

As my body stiffened, I knew I had to see him. More than anything on earth, I had to see him, to speak to him, to reassure as in other days.

"It will hurt too much. Don't go in." I heard the caring words and rejected them.

Inside, I don't know how I got to the right corridor. I saw an endless hallway with countless doors on each side. All were precisely alike except for a single one which, to my eyes, might have been bordered in neon. Shaking myself free, I was drawn to it like a bit of metal responding to the tug of a magnet. I cannot explain this, I cannot understand this, but the image still burns in my mind when I close my eyes. When I opened that door, I knew exactly who I would find.

My son lay on an operating table and his naked body was covered by a sheet and connected by tubes and wires to a whirring machine. As I entered a nurse moved forward protectively. I saw Mitch's chest moving in the rhythmic fluctuations of normal inspiration and aspiration. "He's not dead," I exulted, "He's breathing!"

She said, "Your husband thought that you'd probably join him in giving permission for his kidneys to be used by someone else who needs them. We're trying to save them by keeping his blood circulating. The machine makes it look like he's breathing."

She had meant to be kind, but her words dealt me a mortal blow. Of course his kidneys could be used where they would help another life, but this meant that my son was unmistakably dead, lying there naked beneath a hospital sheet, inhaling fake breaths in a mechanical parody of breathing.

I needed to touch him, to stroke his lifeless arm, to imprint the reality of his death on my brain . . . on my heart. I needed that moment to hold my son and to say goodbye.

6   MY SON ... MY SON ...

A thin bracelet encircled his right wrist, a silver band of the sort teenage youths wear. I became aware of the need to remove it. I stepped to his side and unlocked it, gently took it from his cooling skin, and stepped back into the arms of my husband. Reluctantly, I could now leave. I had delivered Mitch into this world wholly nude and now he would depart exactly as he came. Holding his bracelet in my hand, I felt connected to my dead son. Clinging to this treasure, I backed out of the room, fearing that I might never see him again.

When we left the hospital that afternoon, I felt like an empty husk, drained of substance. I was stunned into robot-like movement even though I'd been spared the interrogation of physicians, hospital personnel, and police officers by the intervention of my husband. Later I would learn that the stresses they imposed would be minuscule compared to those that would come soon.

At home again, I felt compelled to go straight to Mitch's room. Its consistent messiness had become all too familiar. I needed to see where he had fallen or collapsed, where he was lying when Jack discovered him.

Parenthetically, my husband and our neighbor, Norm, had been enjoying a morning coffee break in our kitchen when Mitch had breezed past them with a jocular comment and greeting. They had detected no unusual strain in his voice or demeanor. Without pausing, he had gone on to his room.

Some time later, the family phone had rung—we had installed a second instrument for our sons—and a girl (I'll call her Jane) told Jack, "I've been talking to Mitch on the other line and something's happened. There was an awful sound. Could you go to his room and see if he's okay?"

My husband responded immediately and found Mitch unconscious, sprawled on his bed, bleeding from two bullet wounds, one in his temple, the second, from another gun, in his mouth. Jack called an ambulance and the police. Then he tried to find me at the meeting I had attended that morning, but I had left. The ambulance came and rushed Mitch to the hospital. Jack and the boys followed. Norm waited for me. He wanted to dispose of the bloody mattress. Neighbors had been loading it into a truck when I turned into our driveway.

As I recall, when I entered the hallway that led to Mitch's bedroom, it was still too early to accept the reality of his death, which seems to be characteristic of many bereaved parents. As illogical as I now know it to be, I really expected to find him in his room. In grief I soon learned that the mind plays many such tricks. So I sped along the passageway to his closed door. A yellow sheet of paper had been taped to it that said, "Do not enter." It bore the no-nonsense signature of our household helper, Virginia. For reasons unknown then or now, I was suddenly stunned by this exclusion. I instinctively knew that I had to face that room immediately. Ripping the sign from the door, I turned the knob and crossed the threshold. Within, I was shocked by the almost antiseptic tidiness which had been imposed on what must have been a bloody chaos. Instead of the familiar bed, its covers in familiar lumps and swirls, I saw naked springs, boxed and muslined as if in a warehouse. In her great heart, Virginia had not wanted me to be hurt by the sight of reddened towels and clothes in disarray, so she had scrubbed, vacuumed, dusted, and Air-wicked. My son was truly gone, even his scent. Except for two things: a glass of iced tea from which he had been drinking—tea was never far from his hand—stood three-quarters full on a bedside table just as he had left it. And a book about the English author Thomas Hardy.

Later, I was to learn that my anger had prompted me to a helpful response. If I had not opened that door and stormed inside, I now know that grief authorities believe I might have fallen into the error made by so many bereaved parents who turn their beloved child's bedchamber into a shrine. Too often they freeze each object in place, wherever it was when death called, which simultaneously freezes the process of grieving so that one is condemned forever after to bear an intolerable burden. They permit no changes in the posters and pictures on the wall, no laundering of jackets in the closet, nor do they allow any change within their own emotional structure that could dilute the pain of what might become an obsessional grief.

That I escaped such a fate was sheer luck. Though I was aware of suicide as a horrid death chosen by a growing number of youths, I had no idea of the power of its seductive appeal. Nobody had told me that approximately 35,000 Americans had killed themselves in a single year. And that many experts believed that at least 250,000 other citizens had attempted it during that same span.

Nor was the remainder of the world any different. The stark, unsuspected truth was that somewhere on this earth about 1,000 hapless humans were destroying themselves every single day.

In this country, the body count was running at the rate of 100 kids, 14 to 19 years of age, every week. Even more frightening was the fact that teenage suicides have escalated by 250 percent during the last decade.

Would I have acted differently as a mother if I had known such things? Honestly, I do not know. What is clear to me is that every parent needs all the knowledge he or she can muster to combat the death-wish of our pressurized sons and daughters. We need to know more facts and we need to be able to recognize clues. Such as, for instance, the presence of a gun in a son's room which might be the tell-tale indication of some internal desperation. Males, as I have learned, usually use a noose or firearms, while females often prefer pills or poison.

A significant forerunner, I have been told by authorities, is a sense of loss. This might be the loss of a job, of a girl friend, of a spouse, even of a skill diminished by bad health or the passage of time. I think of David Garroway who died rich and admired but who had lost his status as a celebrity. I think of the bank officer in a small town who was discovered rifling his bank's vault, and who shot himself. He had lost his status. I think also of the death of Marilyn Monroe who, it is said, had lost a lover.

Apparently, the self gradually dissolves when the anxiety and pressures of an irreplaceable loss are imposed. When this occurs, the present becomes laced with pain and the future becomes intolerable. This state of mind is sometimes called depression. Physicians say it is commonly among the first symptoms of suicide.

The day that Mitch died, as I recall, I experienced no depression. Later, it would hit me hard and I would wonder if Mitch had felt it. If he did, he never showed it but apparently masked it, as many youths do. My own reaction was a numbness that reduced me to automatic responses and a total feeling of personal unworthiness. To climb from that emotional abyss, though I did not know it, would force me to fight the hardest battle of my life.

3
Formula for Survival

At this juncture, I knew nothing and cared less that the twentieth century had brought a new kind of understanding of the age-old scandal of suicide. Sigmund Freud, of Vienna, was its godfather. Freud combined elements of psychology, physiology, plus his own unique perceptions of the human psyche. Suicide, he said, was the result of mankind's inner compulsions. Emotions, he said, were the source of the secret forces that drive men into extreme reactions. It was man's natural estate to be driven mostly by twin drives: the first drive was to survive, the second was to die. His theory made every human being, given the right conditions, a prospective suicide. Given enough stress, he maintained, the ego would be overwhelmed and the death wish would win.

Psychiatrist Karl Menninger had gone even further. He said that a person who attempts suicide is dominated by either a wish to kill or a wish to be killed or a wish to die. In other words, such a person is full of hate. Some specialists assert that the wellsprings of self-hate are helplessness and hopelessness, plus rejection by a person of major importance. Karen Horney, specializing in children, says the first step toward suicide originates in anxiety. Being anxious, the child sees the world as a hostile place. Unable to cope, the child develops deep-rooted feelings of inferiority. From there, everything goes downhill.

What does it all mean? America's most experienced practicing suicidologist, Dr. Edwin Shneidmann, says, "There is no simple formula." Important factors, he says, are anguish, pain, impotent rage, shame, guilt, and frustrated dependency—the latter especially.

Another element, one that emerges from all the others, he calls "isolated desperation." In his candid words, "the person involved has been positioned into a dark corner where there is no hope (by way of human communication or contact) of relief. There is no one to turn to."

All these theorists were unknown to me when I needed them most. Fortunately, my own determination to understand what had happened, and the words of good friends who were willing to help, provided the support I needed to survive my worst moments. Learning slowly and hurting badly, I discovered that grief and recovery from its malignancy are a process and that experts had broken it down into a number of steps, a kind of roadmap of what to expect. It is common for all these phases to occur but a number of people experience only some of them.

The first three stages are usually shock, denial, and bargaining. They may come in sequence, one after the other, or all at once. Working through them (in my case, I call it suffering through them) took me several months.

Shock is hard to describe; call it a mixture of numbness and disbelief.

Denial is when you wake up in the morning and momentarily have forgotten that anything has happened. All of a sudden, it hits you in the face, in the heart, in your arms and legs like a paralytic stroke. Denial is also meeting your son on the street, seeing him from behind, the same shaped head, the identical droop of the shoulders, the swinging gait. Your leaping heart cries, "Oh, it's Mitch!" Some days, you'll walk into the house and "feel" his presence in a room. You can "see" that smile, "hear' his laugh. A part of my denial was setting the table for him. Time and again, I'd set his place with all the others and then gasp under the realization that he would never be coming home to dinner.

Bargaining may be talking with God, or with the wind, or promising never to err again, never to do anything wrong. You think, "Oh God, just bring him back." Sometimes you pray with such force that you actually believe that he will be brought back.

Guilt is perhaps the most punishing stage of all. I remember that first day sitting on my bed saying over and over, "What have I done wrong? If only I had done more." My senses told me that I'd failed as a parent, failed myself, failed my son, failed my profession. The word I used to describe my condition was foul. Irrationally I thought I must indeed be foul for my son to prefer death to living with me and our family. Guilt hits hard and flits in and out of other moods.

Anger is rage at the world, at myself, at God, eventually at my son himself, at the fact that other young men are playing tennis but not my Mitch, at the unfairness of life that unreasoned choices must be accepted without question. In grief, injustice is a very tender spot. I remember that we had no good photo of Mitch except a small one that had been taken during his older brother's wedding. We asked the photographer if we could buy the negative. When he refused, I was so hurt that I cried for hours, and then became insanely angry at his callousness. My reaction was normal, I learned.

Resignation is the realization of the fact that what has happened is permanent and real. Finally you believe it. Acceptance, the following stage, is almost identical. Now you know it happened and it can't be changed. Once you are resigned, you face up to reality. Acceptance is admitting that you must make a decision about your future. You can't change destiny, but you can take charge of how you respond.

To these stages, I have added hope because ultimately one does begin to hope. Hope treads lightly at first, but as time passes its steps become firmer. My mail often contained cheering letters that said, "You're going to make it." Hope is the product of people who wish you well. I was invited by A. B. Padgett, a close friend, to make a speech before a local Rotary Club. I said, "Do you really think I can?" For a long time, I had dreaded even showing my face in public.

"You have more to say now than ever before," he replied. "Of course, you can." He was right. How greatly a bereaved mother needs friends to help create hope.

I have not mentioned the stage called depression—the English poets called it melancholia—because it is really more of a constant companion, lurking within your psyche for days and then springing like a wolf at your throat because of some slight, or the breaking of a shoe lace or even the stubbing of a toe. Its lease on its lair in your subconscious can endure for years. Its antidote, I learned, is contact with people who care.

4
A Promise I Can't Believe

But none of these matters were in my consciousness that afternoon of Day One. A glance through the window showed cars turning into our driveway. Friends were walking across the lawn. Someone asked me, "Do you really want to see anyone this afternoon?"

"Oh, I do. I really need to see them," I replied. Perhaps I needed neighbors and loved ones around me to assure me I would survive, that in spite of this abomination I would still have loving and accepting friends, and life would go on. Also it is my nature to be a caregiver, and it is my profession. Instinct told me that many of those arriving would need my care and love as much as I needed theirs. Perhaps we could help each other. I had no idea what to say or do until I walked into their midst, eyes brimming, arms extended, and through those next painful hours, one by one, those friends taught me things that are a vital part of life but never discussed in higher education. Or anywhere else.

Society still fears a suicidal person, whether he is alive or dead. Invariably, he is a puzzle and a menace because he personifies the ultimate nonconformist. He is also a seducer. If his demise seems to prove that death is more to be desired than life, then it is assumed that many other troubled souls will be encouraged to follow his example.

Most words, I quickly discovered, were for good times, not bad. Even some well-chosen words, I learned, could be as wracking as torture. "It was God's will," "I know how you feel," "Some day you'll know it was for the best," and "Everything is going to be all right." Such pleasantries flicked my emotions like a cat-o-nine-tails. My guilt-ridden mind screamed back at them, "Everything's *not* going to be all right. What can you know of my hurt or my disaster? Have you ever lost a child by suicide?" But how we hugged each other. An aphorism came to mind: "One hug is worth a thousand words." We embraced silently, caringly, and strongly, and in those embraces a miracle came to pass. My numbness lessened as my frozen nerve ends began to thaw. Then, someone said, "Life isn't fair," and I knew they understood.

For hours, I recall that doorbells buzzed and phones rang and, presently, every chair was occupied and friends and strangers were sitting on the floor. A suicide in a home is a surprise package. It is a bomb tossed through a transom, that rips your door off its hinges and admits an army of invaders including newspaper reporters, TV cameramen, the curious, the sensation seekers, cemetery salesmen, undertakers, and tombstone promoters. Miraculously, a combat force of old and new friends, family members, ministers, and colleagues emerged to take charge. With relief and gratitude, I temporarily relinquished to them the care and feeding of my soul. But my thoughts race ahead.

Many other friends are out of sight at the end of long distance phone lines and air routes. Wherever they are, they deserve to be told what has happened. Grandparents, uncles, aunts and cousins must be notified as quickly as possible. Friends and neighbors who have shared the drama of your birthings and parenting also deserve the right to share in this ultimate cataclysm.

What had happened is that my family room had suddenly become a battlefield. Dimly, I perceived that this was the ground on which I would either lose or win my fight for survival. Only within this home, I somehow knew, could my foundation of self-confidence be built anew. On one hand, I saw myself as a beaten-down and fragmented mother whose best efforts had failed. On the other hand, I saw the surrounding army of a society in which suicide was a disgrace, perhaps a sign of insanity more often than a cowardly cop out, and which places on all relatives—especially the mother—the stigma of iniquity. The one-sidedness of this fantasy made me reel. In my section of Atlanta, I was known as the director of The Link Counseling Center, a private, non-profit, community-based headquarters for family therapy. For years, distrait families had shared their pain with me and our staff when their kids had run away or been addled by drugs or stiffened by alcoholism. I was a problem solver of family dilemmas. I was a woman with insights and alternatives, and now I had none for myself. I had flunked the supreme test of motherhood, the delivery of a self-confident, valuable citizen to society. Instead, I had delivered a corpse.

Gone now from his retreat at the end of the hall, Mitch was now only a cipher, destroyed, I feared, by some failure of my mothering, my relationship with him, or by some neglect in apportioning my time between his needs and my other interests. I had failed, failed. And I felt foul, foul, foul. . . .

Friends told me later that I had borne myself that first day with apparent bravery, talking, welcoming, even smiling. They did not guess that I was numb, devastated, embarrassed, and secretly wishing for my own death. But how their loving presence sustained me.

The interminable afternoon passed slowly. I became amazed and finally bewildered at the solicitude of visitors I hardly knew, and of the universal panacea for pain that many recommended. Wanting to help, some of them dug into purses or vest pockets for small packets of pills which they pressed into my hand, saying, "These things keep me going. They'll settle you down. Take two."

Others said, "I've left a bottle in the kitchen. Let me mix you a stiff drink." I finally opened a bottle of wine to forestall their well-meant entreaties, and stood with a glass in my hand. I'm told that I eventually emptied that container of its entire content, but I recall no effect. No drug, no amount of alcohol could erase this event from my mind. The pain remained, lodged in my entrails like a fishhook.

Being responsibly involved in the repair of shattered psyches and fractured egos requires one's own self-help. Most professionals feel this is important. One of the most beloved and respected psychiatrists in Atlanta is Leonard T. Maholick, M.D., P.C., a skilled psychotherapist and a dear friend.

When he arrived that Saturday afternoon, he offered no trite panaceas. We had readily established the kind of warm relationship that is essential for any kind of emotional healing. I had given him my trust and there was mutual respect between us. I am enthusiastic, he is calm. I am mercurial, he is rock steady. How I needed his help. My husband joined us and we left our mourning guests and made our bedroom a private sanctuary. Once the conventional remarks had been said, Doctor Maholick made it clear that we might expect to be in an emotional shock for a while, which would give way presently to moments of denial or bargaining or guilt. Inevitably, we would also experience anger and depression. These stages of grief, so to speak, came with the territory. And then he added an extra dimension to his counseling that seemed at that moment to be utterly beyond belief. "I ask you to hold two things in your mind. The first thing," the doctor said, "is that this crisis can be used to bring your family closer together than ever. If you use this opportunity wisely, you can survive and be a stronger unit than before."

"But how?" I asked.

"The formula is simple. Make every decision together throughout this crisis. Hear every voice. Work for a consensus. Never exclude your children during these next few days. Call family conferences. Discuss each problem openly, treating each individual equally regardless of age or experience. Today, each of you is hurting in his own unique way. You can blame each other and destroy one another. Or you can share and be supportive. Grief of itself is a medicine when you are open about it. Only secret grief is harmful. Through mutual helping, you will all heal more rapidly, and you will all survive. The choice is yours."

I had never heard of such a doctrine but it made sense. Family integrity and unity had been the foundation stone of our lives. Jack and I nodded in agreement.

"The second thing is more difficult to grasp," he continued carefully. "You have no reason as yet to believe what I am going to tell you, but I ask you to hear me with an understanding heart. There is a gift for you in your son's death. You may not believe it at this bitter moment, but it is authentic and it can be yours if you are willing to search for it. To other eyes it may remain hidden. The gift is real and precious and you can find it if you choose."

I gasped! He was saying that my pain was a gift, that the dislocation of so many lives caused by my son's careless and selfish termination of all earthly responsibilities, was a gift. I saw in memory the naked body on the hospital table, felt the smoothness of his dead skin as I removed his bracelet, and I fantasized his head being ripped by bloody bullet trails and his body stripped of its kidneys. Was this doctor saying *that* was a *gift?*

"Mitch has damaged you grievously," he continued, "but he was a good person and a thinking person and he did only what he had to do for reasons that must have appealed to him. Within those reasons there had to be some degree of awareness of the problem he felt he had become to himself, to his friends, and to this family. So he did what he felt he had to do, and in doing it, he gave you a gift." The words I was hearing were incredible. Could I believe them? I recalled Oscar Wilde's writing, "I can believe in anything so long as it is incredible."

"This gift will not jump out at you or thrust itself into your life," Maholick continued. "You must search for it. As time passes, you will be amazed at unanticipated opportunities for helping yourself and others that will come your way, all because of Mitch. Today, you probably need to condemn him. It's only natural. But I earnestly believe that one day you will be able to acknowledge his gift."

My husband grimaced. "I hear your words, but they have no meaning for me."

"That's okay. Perhaps one day they will," Maholick said gently.

5
Healing Begins at Home

Our minister provided the initial testing of Dr. Maholick's theory. It concerned the disposition of Mitch's body. "What is your desire?" he asked. "Do you prefer cremation or burial?"

Suddenly, we were faced with the reality of state and city laws regarding corpses, with the economics of embalming, plus the prospect of dozens of other decisions pressing for immediate answers. Cremation or burial? We had never thought of either. What family has?

Jack and I called a family meeting in our bedroom, including Mitch's ex-girl-friend with whom he had apparently been talking when he pulled the trigger. On the floor, on the bed, or standing, we somehow gradually became something quite different from the half-dozen or so separate sufferers who had been awkwardly receiving the condolences of visitors. Here, we were a family, a unit with roots running back through all eternity and through all the families that had used their united strength to face down all the misfortune of history. Unanimously, we agreed that Mitch should be buried in a beautiful nearby cemetery.

When our little meeting was concluded, I felt good. I felt love all around me. Everyone felt it. We were a *force* again.

Len Maholick had spoken wisely. We had made a beginning, and I sensed a wisp of improvement in my own spirit: a sense of an umbrella-like symbol of hope over my head, that perhaps I would survive.

All three of my sons were a support to my numbed being. My eldest son John, 22, with his strong arms always open for a reassuring hug, his care of his younger brothers, his take-charge manner, and his protectiveness of me—these are my remembrances of him. His wife, Kathy, was always there, loving, helping, caring. Bill, 16, was by my side asking, "Are you okay, Mom?" His loving concern was evident in his tortured eyes as he hugged me, patted my shoulder or bravely welcomed guests. Bobby, 14, was sensitive to my every need and to the needs of others. He checked regularly to see what he could do to help, in spite of his own pain.

That night I ached from my toes to the top of my head. Jack rubbed my back with loving tenderness. Alone, we simply held each other closely, but there was no sleep.

The following day became a wasteland. I was barely conscious of being surrounded by friends and loving relatives who supplied every need. Devoted associates from my office manned the phone. Jack's mother and my mother became house managers, cooks and advisors. Friends organized taxi-service from the airport, and arranged lodging. My sister Lynn turned hostess, confidante, and traffic cop. That first night, guests had filled the house until shortly before sunrise. Jack's father and mine stood tall and calm.

One afternoon, a handsome youth with the brown skin and brown eyes of ancient India knocked on our door. He was a student in an Atlanta university and had met Mitch playing tennis in the park; he had invited him to a concert and had come to pick him up. When we told him that Mitch was dead, he was stunned. His eyes closed and his body seemed to wilt. "But why? I don't understand. I can't believe it. I thought I'd found a friend." We clung to each other for long minutes and then he departed.

Other complications involved choosing a casket. Mitch detested ostentation. Many other observers have documented the unfortunate tactics that have so often been imposed on numbed parents. I shall say only that Mitch was buried in a handsome, pine box that we discovered in the corner of a casket dealer's showroom despite some opposition, after persistent search.

The viewing of Mitch's body at the mortuary was less traumatic. Our family had met again and reached a decision that we owed an open coffin visit to Mitch's friends as well as to ourselves. Mitch had committed suicide but Mitch did not look like a suicide. The team of morticians had seen to that. Nor did he look much like Mitch except in a blurred kind of way. But he was handsomely cosmetized and showed no sign of a wound.

Our family looked at his face in silence for a long time, and then Jack and I and the three boys moved on. After all the others had seen him, I returned and stood by his body for a last personel visit. I knew that I did not look much like Iris Bolton, either, with my blurred, tear-swollen features, but I had to respond to a call from somewhere that told me that my presence there beside him was vital to my future.

So I took my place at his head, not crying, not even thinking, but just being there. For reasons unknown, that farewell moment gave me an extraordinarily peaceful feeling. My tarrying must have lasted too long because someone stepped forward and tugged at my elbow. I shook him off. He returned, exerting more strength. To my amazement, I jerked my arms free. "I'm not ready yet!" Such assertiveness was foreign to my nature but now it was the product of a growing awareness that many others were assuming that they knew what was best for me.

"It's time to move on," this "other" had obviously decided. But it was not time to move on by my chronometer. I still had unfinished business to do with my son. I was learning that a mourning female, more frequently than not, must fend for herself, make her own judgments of her inner needs, and act on them, if she is not to be protected and treated as a helpless woman.

When my needs had been met, whatever they were in that extended moment of mourning, I was finally ready to move to the final ritual act. I studied that dear face for the last time, painting its features on a mental canvas composed of axons and neurons and dendrites, weaving them indelibly into memory. I leaned down and kissed his forehead. Then, part mother and part priest, I whispered, "Goodbye, Mitch. God holds you now," and closed the coffin with my own hands.

6
The Magic of a Dream

My son had left an open book beside his bed. Its author, H. C. Duffin, wrote about the works of Thomas Hardy. Underlined in red was the following passage:

> It was in his nature to do it. The doctor says there are such boys springing up amongst us—boys of a sort unknown in the last generation—the outcome of new views of life. They seem to see all its terrors before they are old enough to resist them. He says it is the beginning of the coming universal wish not to live.

An old high school book report also lay on the bedside table. In his senior year, Mitch had written, "Hardy recognizes the fact that death is imminent and is the only real end of depression, pain and failure. Hardy's novels show death often as a cruel end of life, but also as a long awaited relief from continuing stress. For Jude, one of Hardy's characters, death may have brought relief or a letting go of the vicious cycle of failures in his life. Jude's offspring, Little Father Time, is in a way an illustration of Hardy's view of life. Little Father Time's insight to life showed him that life only leads to death, so suicide seemed to be the only logical end." His teacher's comment written on the front page of the report said, "A beautiful paper. Brilliant reading and writing—A-Plus."

22   MY SON ... MY SON ...

Having read these writings and several despairing poems by Hardy, I received another gift, or so I believe, three nights after his death. Some hours before dawn, I arose from a restless sleep, sick to my stomach. When I got back to bed, I must have dozed because I began to hear words and phrases that fitted together like poetry.

The words of a poem rushed into my ears as I lay there. I felt that I had to copy them before they vanished. It was as if I had to get the sickness out of my body and so my flesh was reacting. My husband was asleep for the first time in three nights, so I slipped out of bed and rushed to the den and started writing. The verses continued to come in alternate bouts of pressure and release. It was like giving birth and vomiting at the same time. Waves of hope and despair swept over me as I scribbled. I wrote as one taking dictation. Gradually the pace slowed and finally there was silence. I was physically and emotionally exhausted. It was dawn and the poem was finished, or so I thought.

Later, awake and grateful for a renewed sleep, I soaked in a hot tub, still in awe of the night's experience. Suddenly, I became aware of the sound of piano music. It filled the room and saturated my mind. It was a tape recording made by my son Mitch that I had never heard. He had been a musician, composing, playing and singing his own work. After his death, his brothers had found the tape beside the piano on his recorder. They had told me of this new composition but I had not had the courage to hear it. It was the last recording he would ever make and I wasn't sure I could handle it. Now it flooded the bathroom with glorious sounds, a gift made golden when my son Bill had put the tape on his player in his bedroom immediately below.

As the melody swept to a triumphant climax, I was seized by its beauty, and my spirit soared, lifted by the exhilaration of the moment. Immediately, the words that I had heard earlier in my dream returned. Miraculously, they fitted the cadence I was hearing. As I listened again, I realized that my dream-poem had omitted any mention of one of the most important aspects of Mitch's life, which was his music. He had fought for its perfection and its acceptance, and perhaps this is also why he had died. Now new words were thundering in my head exactly as they had during my dream-writing. I had brought my pad and pencil to the bath with me. Again, as if taking dictation, I wrote what I heard. Finally, when I had four additional verses, the word flow stopped. The poem was finished.

Now it spoke of my son's music, a subject untouched by the dream-writing of the previous night. A sense of satisfaction, completeness, and healing came over me with the union of poetry and music. I felt it was a labor of love, and a gift.

I am not a poet and have never experienced such a moment of inspiration before or since. My best efforts have been inept attempts to versify my allegedly humorous birthday wishes to friends and relatives. But this nocturnal elegy was something else. And perhaps something important. Several years later, I continue to be astounded at some of those words.*

> My son lies cruel and cold today.
>   He'll never touch another;
> My son lay kind and warm before;
>   I know—I am his mother.
>
> His troubled heart, his bleeding soul,
>   His tortured body lies,
> Yet lived he twenty years today,
>   And now he's closed his eyes.

In the poem I seem to have spoken directly to him:

> My son, my son, how came you here?
>   What answers did you seek?
> Alas, you listened not, my dear.
>   Did you not hear me speak?
>
> I knew your selfish pride, my son,
>   Perfection was your goal;
> If only you had learned, my love,
>   That failure makes you whole.

Then, bursting out of my subconscious was Dr. Maholick's unbelievable prophecy of a gift:

> A gift, I'm told, you've left behind,
>   That I must seek and find;

> But pain too deep and missing you,
>   Have blocked my open mind.
>
> I wonder if the gift you've left
>   Will ever be revealed;
> Or still is locked inside your soul,
>   Eternally concealed.

Surprisingly, my concern for other parents surfaced, which came, I suspect, from my long sessions at our **Link Counseling Center.**

> I ache for other mothers, too,
>   Across this land of ours,
> Whose troubled sons must all be helped
>   Before their new wine sours.
>
> Let's not ask why—no answer comes—
>   Instead, let's study how
> We can prevent their useless deaths.
>   Let mankind do it now.

And finally:

> If pain and torment, wave on wave,
>   Will ever leave my soul,
> O God, I pray what's left of me,
>   Will once again be whole.

*(See Appendix A for the entire poem)

Even now, years later, with the mysterious processes of grief almost wholly worked through, I cannot begin to explain why those words echoed through my mind.

Of one element of this mystery, I have absolutely no doubt. The poem was a gift which enabled me, very early in the healing process, not only to help myself but also to begin to help others. When it was read to similarly bereaved mothers, some of them asked for copies. One mother has told me she read it at bedtime every night for months. Another said, she felt hope for the first time in years.

The euphoria of that morning did not last long. The day of

the funeral came and went in a blur of feelings. There were hours when I wanted to die. My mood must have showed because, following the burial, Dan Mermin, Ph.D., an old friend and co-worker in the counseling field, said to me, "A time may come when you'll simply want to talk to somebody. If it does, know that you have only to phone me. I'll meet you, day or night. And know that someday you may need to get angry at Mitch. You may want to be alone then or you might want someone with you. All you have to do is call."

How right he was.

7
The Ups and Downs of Grief

My previous concept of the period following a funeral was that things would simmer down, one's grief would lessen, life would become normal. I was in for many surprises. Mitch's girl friends, for instance. There were several, each of them experiencing her own pain and devastation and wanting my time and attention.

When my other sons returned to their school classes, they immediately encountered the stigma of being the brother of one who had killed himself. The facts of Mitch's death had been exaggerated and a rumor had spread that he had shot up his bedroom like a drunken cowboy in a western film. The word was passed that he had even threatened the life of another student. My boys faced these lies and then joined the remainder of the family in healing rap sessions.

Trying to strike a balance, we learned to call things by their right name and to admit that Mitch had been a very human mix of tenderness and tantrums. He always helped the down and out, befriending kids who had run away or who had no place to go. My training in psychology prevented any inclination to turn him into a super-son or to build a shrine. This viewpoint encouraged our other sons to talk about his habit of bursting into a placid family circle, setting one brother against the other with preposterous tales, and then leaving the scene with a laugh while they fought among themselves.

Nor was he generous in frustration or defeat. Son Billy had played tennis with him one night at a court over a mile from home. He recalled, "When I beat him, and I think it was the first time I'd ever beaten him, he was so mad he got in the car and refused to let me ride with him. It was midnight and I had to walk home."

Thus, we healed day by day but it was very, very slow.

Our informal conversations prevented another disaster, which is scapegoating. Human nature normally shrinks from self-blame and tries to pin the onus on someone else. When a suicide occurs, this can become epidemic. The parents blame each other. One son blames another, a parent, or any handy target. Then after you have blamed everyone else, as well as yourself, you understand perhaps that there must be other answers. So you share the blame with the person himself who completed the suicide. You say, "I have blamed myself and everybody else, but that is obviously not the answer. There are no answers, but the responsibility really lies with the person himself." My struggle was this: On one hand, I could empathize with pain so overwhelming that death seemed the only way out. On the other hand, my anger said, "How dare you do this to those who love you."

Finally, I saw that my son's death was his choice. His death was *his* responsibility, exactly as it would have been had he taken the life of any other human. Dan was right. When I understood that, I could get angry and place some of the blame for our turmoil and pain on his shoulders. That was the key to my emancipation from scapegoating. We carried this understanding into our family sessions, and our slow healing continued.

Mornings were the worst time. The agony they brought upon awaking was intense. For a while, I thought such pain must be the embodiment of some special punishment God had designed for my failures. It never occurred to me that any other person on earth had ever suffered similarly. Months later I read *The Bereaved Parent,* by Harriet Sarnoff Schiff, and discovered that I was not alone. She had written:

> Far worse than lying awake all night were the mornings. Then, like a tidal wave, remembrance would come and assault me and

make me think I was drowning. I had to fight my way out of bed every day. This went on for several months. This was probably my toughest battle. Nothing in life can be more emotionally draining.... If it takes all that energy to get up, what energy is left for the day.

I wish I had known that sooner.

My hope for a settling-down period was not to be realized. Although the support of many friends was constant, a few friends began to avoid me, crossing to the other side of the street when a meeting impended, or contributing banal aphorisms when we met face to face. I remember hearing a lot about "seeing things through" from persons who had no conception of my trauma. At the time, I assumed that their apparent disdain signaled a repudiation of our friendship and a confirmation that I was a total failure. I did not know until later that some people cannot handle the fact of death, and flee from anyone who reminds them of the painful subject. I didn't know that some people empathize so strongly that they can't stand to face the bereaved.

Inevitably, I was forced to visit our grocery store to buy food for our family. Driving to and fro, I developed the feeling that my car bore a huge sign reading, "My son committed suicide. I am a failure." At the store, I would load my shopping cart and then my eyes would fall on some item of food or drink that had been Mitch's favorite. Then the bottom would drop out of my day and I would be forced to abandon my cart and rush to the parking lot before tears dissolved my self-control.

Months earlier, I had been named a candidate for an award, given by the Atlanta Jaycee Singles group, called the "Leading Ladies of Atlanta." It was an honor to be nominated. Later, a half-dozen winners would be chosen from the panel of nominees. When a friend brought me the news that I had been designated for this coveted award I could not comprehend it. "Don't they know what's happened?" I protested. "I'm not a leading lady. I'm a failed parent and a discredited counselor. Go tell them that."

I mention these details to show how deeply depressed and guilty I had become. During that awful fortnight following the funeral, I suffered deeply from human nature's most puzzling blight, the condition called depression.

8
The Secret Anatomy of Depression

Depression is probably the most common symptom encountered in counseling. Almost everyone suffers from it at one time or another. Working as a counselor, I had often discovered it in others. Now I experienced it personally, indeed, was overwhelmed by it. Because the term depression is so imprecise, psychiatrists have tried to clarify it. One such effort has resulted in the Beck Depression Inventory Scale, which is really a checklist of the elements to be encountered in this widely distributed emotional state.

Dr. Beck's roster named sadness, hopelessness, failure, dissatisfaction, guilt, deserved or wanted punishment, self-disgust, self-blame, wanting to die, crying, irritability, loss of interest in others, inability to make decisions, being unattractive or ugly, difficulty working, sleep disturbed, fatigue, poor or no appetite, weight loss of 10 to 15 pounds, preoccupation with health, and loss of interest in sex. Other observers added poor concentration, suicidal ruminations, inability to accept responsibility, and diminished ability to love.

I felt that *my* depression embraced them all.

Yet, even as one part of my mind was numbed into self-contempt, another part continuously puzzled over the last days of Mitch's life. What signs had I missed that would have alerted a caring mother?

Until the twentieth century, the Western World had thought that self-destruction was an act of insanity or a great sinner's final fling. In the seventeenth century, a faint English voice turned things around. It belonged to John Donne, England's celebrated poet and prelate. He wrote a book arguing that suicide might be acceptable to God because his power and mercy were great enough to "remit the sin of suicide." Cannily, he waited until he was dead before allowing his thoughts to be read by the public. Nevertheless, his arguments made sense and other thinkers soon supported his position.

Sociologists were the first scholars to wrest suicide from the devil and give it to the statisticians. A Frenchman named Emile Durkheim published a majestic theory, with vast statistical documentation, proving that society itself was the cause. By counting thousands of noses, he concluded that the tides of self-death rose or ebbed with the general economic status, with the vigor of the economy, and with the location of one's residence. Said Durkheim, two social factors might provide immunity from suicide. The first was integration of a person into the affairs of one's community. The second was submission to the social control of one's family, church, and profession. In short, to live happily ever after, one needed to be a conformist. These many years later, we are only a little further along in discovering the true origins of the desire to die.

After listening to many experts, I finally came to an acceptance of the complex "Three H" formula advanced by Dr. Calvin J. Frederick, of Washington, D. C. He believes that most candidates for suicide are hapless, hopeless, and helpless.

I have often wondered if such usually is the case. Was my son, during his last weeks or days, altogether hapless, hopeless, and helpless? I did not judge him so then, but I cannot help but wonder now.

Earlier by a year, I had met Mitch at a nearby school yard to talk and discovered that he was suffering great emotional pain. He confided his hurts to me as never before, and we sat in the sun and talked for hours. He said, "Mom, I don't want to die, but I can't stand the pain of living." Of my four boys, he was the only one who seemed to be adrift. Then 19, he had chosen not to go to college but to perfect his talent as a writer and singer of songs. His daily sessions at our piano lasted for hours. He had composed many tunes and tried to get them published. Nothing had succeeded, and his appetite for success burned in him like a flame. Hungering for fame, he also feared it. "What if my first album is a blockbuster and sells a million? What can I do for an encore?" he asked friends. It was not an idle question. He had really packed his future into his first writings, and he could not see how anything that might come later could live up to them. The failure of his dream to be a songwriter and entertainer had been a knockout blow. His fear of success and fear of failure apparently immobilized him.

Because of our talk, I was aware of his pain and his fascination with the notion of suicide. Self-destruction was not a panacea for him personally, I concluded, but rather for others in a more desperate plight. When he did a term paper in his senior year on Thomas Hardy's self-destructive literary characters, I regarded it as one of the aberrations of adolescence. On the day of our schoolyard talk, however, I responded to his need by suggesting that he accept professional help, and he agreed. After his fifth visit to a psychiatrist, he protested, "He doesn't help me or tell me anything. He just asks questions. I'm not going back." And he dropped out. I didn't know enough then to encourage him to find someone else to whom he could relate.

Summertimes, Mitch had worked at ordinary vacation jobs. After his graduation, he realized his obligation to earn his own living. Like many others, he drifted for a while. My husband and I consoled ourselves by assuming that he needed more time and would find himself. We were delighted when he announced that he had found an opportunity to work in a program that presented workshops on self-esteem building and motivational attitudes. He was excited and it seemed to be an ideal opportunity to develop his own ego strength and personality and to learn needed skills.

During the year he seemed happy and involved in the program, going to workshops, listening to tapes, learning about conducting and selling the program to business and industry. At the same time, he got a job singing and playing his own music at a lounge near the University of Georgia. Things were looking up.

It would be hard to say what turned the tide from hope to hopelessness. One black cloud that loomed covertly for Mitch was his continuing to live at home, although he sometimes lived with a girl friend. He wanted desperately to support himself, yet he had no income. He disliked being dependent. Another struggle was with relationships, particularly with girls. He always had a steady girl. It was as though his self-esteem depended on that relationship, a security blanket of connectedness without which he could not survive.

Three weeks before his death he and his girl friend broke up. I knew he was in pain. One day I heard him playing the piano as tears rolled down his cheeks. I sat beside him on the piano bench and put my arm around him and said, "It's painful, isn't it?" He nodded and wept as his fingers played the melody. Here again, I missed the clue of his deep depression. It had seemed too normal to be grieving over his lost love.

The week before his death, Mitch and I talked for three hours in a chance encounter as he was leaving to play tennis. I had taken the day off and was at home catching up on household chores. I can't remember how the conversation started, as we often talked for hours about life and love and relationships. But this time was somehow special. Our communication was deep and powerful in that we discussed his grief over breaking up with his girl friend, his confusion over loving several women at the same time, his lack of confidence without a male-female relationship to depend on, and his future dreams of being a star. When he finally left to play tennis, three hours later, I was relieved at his openness and sharing. I felt good about his future and his insights into himself. I was to look back on that talk with thankfulness, knowing that we had shared a special time and that I had given him all the wisdom I had to offer. He had talked, I had listened, our souls had touched, and that knowledge eventually helped me survive.

I also missed another sign that might have changed the course of events. In our busy home, we often communicate through notes left on the kitchen table. After our talk, Mitch left a message that said, "Dear Mom and Dad, thanks for turning a lot of hell into a little bit of heaven."

Naively, I was pleased. I thought he was healing. What I overlooked was the almost certain fact that his message was a plea, perhaps subconscious, for help. Modern suicidologists would call it "a cry for help."

A week before Mitch's death he found a job as a salesman of men's wear in a nearby department store. He hated it. He hated having to urge prospective customers to make purchases. "It makes me a hypocrite," he protested. During that first day, he bent over to lift a package from a lower shelf and the seat of his pants split open. He told about it jokingly, but I recognized the disguise of what had been a humiliating experience.

On Friday night before our black Saturday, he brought home a carton of ice cream. We were all delighted and sat in a happy circle as we consumed his gift. (I have since learned that a person who is about to destroy himself frequently will provide a service or an unusual gift to persons he loves.) When he left our group to go to his room downstairs to get some clothes, my mother's instinct bade me to follow. I had not liked the look in his eyes.

He was on the bottom step and I was about halfway down when I called out, "Mitch, are you all right?" He turned, not smiling, and replied, "No worse than any other time. About the same as always." Hungry for reassurance, I accepted that and did not follow him any farther.

For months, a part of my hurt came from the memory of my turning back that night, from not continuing down the stairs to put my arms around him and to invite him to pour out his misery. I know now that a suicidal person can be helped greatly by a concerned and empathetic listener. I also know now that during a suicidal crisis it is best not to leave the person alone. Talking might have helped Mitch, but I'll never know. Later, talking and talking and *talking* would contribute to my own healing. My guilt would turn to regret. But that night I let him go, and that was the last time I saw him alive.

Afterwards, as I searched for reasons that would answer the riddle of Why, I talked to people who could help reconstruct his last hours. The following morning, Saturday, I learned his self-esteem had suffered a humiliating blow when his boss at the department store had called to ask why he had not come to work. He replied that he was not scheduled until two hours later. He had checked the assignment sheet and was supposed to go to work at 1:00 o'clock in the afternoon. It was only 11:00 a.m. His boss insisted that he was late.

I do not know all that was said but I can understand his chagrin at the implication of irresponsibility and incompetence. His boss apparently was very sure of his facts. Of course the store's printed forms were still unfamiliar to my son and he may have made a mistake. Whether he did or not, he felt humiliated.

Mitch's despair and sense of hopelessness, enhanced by this apparent failure, probably led him to call an ex-girl friend. He told her, "I've just blown my job."

It is only human to want reassurance, and their conversation went on to the subject of their personal relations. Seeking validation of his own worth, he finally asked her, "Who is the most important person in the world to you?"

Not aware of his need, she told me later she had answered as honestly as she could, saying, "To me, *I* am the most important person."

"I can't live with that," he murmured. "I will be a star in the sky and watch over you."

Something in his voice told her that a tragedy impended. A loud sound resounded in her earpiece. Quickly, she called my husband on our second phone line and asked him to look in at Mitch to see if he was all right. It was too late.

For a long time I was obsessed with *why* Mitch had ended his life. I thought that I needed to discover the real cause of his hopelessness. I studied and analyzed what I believed to be his suicide note. It read:

>Love is in my heart.
>Psychology has made me mad
>My hands are steady
>Dramatics seem imperative
>Concerned about others sorrow and pain
>Devoted to my freedom.

> Confused about manhood
> Failures no longer hinder
> Desire to be close to my loved ones.
> Torn for the respect of my lover
> Frightened to let go
> God hold me now.

Finally, I perceived that a death by suicide is the result of factors too numerous to count. I wanted to know why, but I didn't have to have an answer in order to go on living my own life. Even the most experienced and astute investigators are finally forced to make what at best is only an educated guess.

It is important, however, to *ask* why. It is important to *worry* about why, because one finally exhausts possibility after possibility and ultimately one tires of the fruitless search.

Then it is time to let it go and to start healing.

9
Picking Up the Pieces

To resume my account of the weeks following Mitch's death, my anguish was certainly not lessened by hearing that a couple of board members, my employers at our private, non-profit counseling center, had decided that my usefulness as director was over. "If she couldn't help her own son, how can she expect to help anyone else?" are the words in which one opinion had circulated. Some said I had to be considered emotionally disturbed. At best, I was unfit to continue in my job.

The funny thing is that I agreed. So paralyzing is the combination of depression, guilt, and shock that its victim is mentally reduced to a jackstraw, a hollow man, a cipher. This abject stance was soon reinforced for me by the first of two strange dreams.

I dreamed that my body was floating in darkness. An enlarged oval salmon can represented my body with my arms and legs attached to its sides. Although this body was actually myself floating in space, I was able to approach it and look down into myself. The salmon can-body apparently had been blown open from inside, leaving jagged edges of tin around its perimeter. As I looked down into myself, I saw that my can-body was empty, void, a hollow surrounded by cold metal. Seeing it, I had no hope, no will to survive. When I awoke, the fading dream amplified my personal emptiness and aloneness.

"What does it mean?" I wondered all the next day. If the dream was truly a portent, I was utterly unprepared to resume my work. I reviewed the advice I was receiving from friends. Some urged, "You must keep busy." Others insisted that I needed a long rest. "Give yourself six months or a year!" The days passed, misted by guilty feelings, and the nights passed, peopled by characters with pointing fingers and clacking tongues. I became miserable because of my uncertainty about what to do. Deep within, my brain hinted faintly but continually that a decision was required. I did not, I could not, respond.

Almost three weeks later, I had the same dream about my salmon can-body, but with one difference. This time, as I approached this can-body and looked down into myself I saw that its interior was covered by a flesh-colored membrane. Where only cold metal had been, now there was a superstratum of what I can only call protoplasm. I knew that I had begun to heal. When I awoke, I was aware that I had made a decision to survive, that my healing was under way, and that this dream was a sign to me.

Next day, I told my friend and psychiatrist, Len Maholick, of the despair that followed the initial dream, of my inability to mobilize enough energy to make a decision, and then of the renewed life I had seen in my salmon can. He agreed that I was healing.

I told him of my options: to take a short vacation, or to take a long vacation with its disruptive effect on my career.

"What do you want to do?" he asked.

The answer came even before I thought. "I want to go back to work."

But then doubts and fears flooded my mind with a torrent of reasons. Others had taken over my assignments. The staff was upset. I wanted a few days alone with my family on the beach and in the sun. The obstacles seemed overwhelming.

Maholick said, "Are you the director of the center?"

I threw back a salvo of "Yes, buts. . . ."

"Are you the director?" he repeated.

Again, I countered, citing an assortment of "what ifs" and "if onlys". . . .

"Are you the director?" Now he spoke loud and clear.

I was silenced. He would not tell me what to do, but he did force me to the realization of my basic problem, and to a consideration of the option which could lead to the solution that I desired. As the director, I had to *be* the director.

I left his office, found a telephone, and called my secretary. "Call a meeting of the entire staff," I directed. "I want everyone there."

I can still remember that moment. Already, I have mentioned the goblins that filled my mind at night. As I talked, I saw those goblins again, jeering, pointing, laughing obscenely at my human strivings. But as I hung up, my inner eye witnessed their discomfiture. Actually, I could watch the mockery fade from their faces as they stepped backward. And then they vanished totally, scrubbed from my brain by my decision to take charge again. At last, the tide within me had turned, and they knew it.

Next day, at our first meeting in a month, with every staff member present, the conference room was charged with vibrations. There is no doubt in my mind that there are good vibes and bad vibes. These vibes were good. My body was still a casualty to unaccustomed stress and had not responded wholly to my need for strength.

So I simply thanked them for their support through my crisis, and for being there. And then I told them that I was going to the beach for a vacation with my family. I did not mention the very real possibility that our Board of Directors might soon solicit my resignation. They, too, had heard such rumors. I did mention that I was far from healed. They were professionals and knew that I was working my way through the mourning process. Finally, I told them that I would be gone for only one more week and that I would then return as their director.

How I got home, I'll never know. My eyes were blinded by the first happy tears in weeks, released by the memory of my staff's warm response and the realization that, after what had seemed an eternity, I had again taken charge of my life.

10
The Miracle of Renewal

Sea and sand have provided therapy for the mental ills of beleaguered invalids since the beginning of time. My pilgrimage to Florida's Sun Coast provided both time and space for solitary walks and painful introspection. My wound was deep and my resurrection had barely begun when my holiday was over. When I returned to Atlanta, I felt calmer and rested though somewhat apprehensive. To say the least, I was not at all prepared for the astonishing things that soon began to happen.

I had wondered, would my community accept a failed parent as the director of its family counseling center? Our friends and neighbors had been generous with their sympathy, but now would they grant me their trust? Their response was soon demonstrated by the arrival at my office door of other bereaved parents who had lost their children. Some were grieving over recent losses. Others were still haunted, after years of sorrow, by the memories of fatal childhood diseases or automobile wrecks. All were trapped in psychic pain and sought help.

Their agony, added to my own, introduced me to a need I had never suspected, and this understanding became the precursor of a change in the direction of my professional life.

Among my other concerns was my wonder—shared by our staff members at The Link—if my son's suicide would affect the legitimacy of our image as healers. Some persons had declared openly that The Link was finished if I were to return. But we continued to be busy. Parents began to refer teenagers to me for help in preventing their suicides, and I was overwhelmed with the wonder of it. How could they think that I might help them when I had failed to save my own son? I was in awe of what seemed to be a miracle. More than anything else, it helped me to begin to find some meaning in the meaninglessness of Mitch's death.

One family brought a youth to me who had shown great promise as a painter in oils. He had reached such a level of hopelessness that he took a brush and a can of black paint and defaced every one of his pictures. This was his way, I learned, of communicating his pain to his parents. It was not really a declaration of self-extinction; rather, it was his cry for help.

A high school girl came to us in a state of crisis, referred by school authorities to whom she had stated her determination to destroy herself; her parents were getting a divorce. Our sympathetic probing revealed that she really did not want to die but had subconsciously turned to the threat of suicide as a desperate plea to her father and mother to remain together. We engaged the whole family in counseling and helped them to an understanding of each other's needs. The divorce was not prevented, but when the mother and daughter moved to their own apartment, both of them were strong enough to meet the challenges of their new life.

Later, a sad and guilt-ridden young woman came to us. She had started her younger brother on drugs and then her brother had committed suicide. Now, our client wanted to do the same. Understandably, she considered herself to be an utterly despicable human being without a single redeeming feature. My task was to assist her in discovering for herself that she was not bad; indeed, that her life was worth saving. Helping a client build a good self-image is never easy. As she identifies her strengths, acknowledges her legitimate guilt and anger as well as her ability to work through those emotions, hope for her survival eventually may lead to her decision to live.

Working with others has always been a tonic for me, but even so there were some difficult days when, for no logical reason, I would fall into an abyss of despair. Walking through a store, the sight of a face that looked like Mitch could trigger a fit of weeping that I could not control. Or the sound of a voice. Or, even more astonishing to me, the "feeling" that he was in the room with me, standing or sitting or watching.

One long, tiring day, the pastor of a local church asked me if I would talk with some of the women of his congregation who had been grieving over the loss of their own loved ones. I had turned down an earlier invitation but now I felt that I had healed enough to share my experience with others.

One evening we met—this was about six months after Mitch's death—and I discovered that grief is an almost universal affliction. We began as a group of a dozen or so but as time passed many others joined us. In the mental health field, such a band as we became might be called a support group. The name is appropriate, for each of us needed support and we each provided support. And we continued to meet regularly for we had found a place where we could talk freely and express our deepest feelings. It was a revelation to listen to people who had mourned a death for years, thinking all the while that they were slightly crazy or, at the very least, peculiar and spineless. They told of sleeping in a dead husband's pajamas, of refusing to remove his razor from the medicine cabinet, of regularly renewing the perfume a daughter had left on her dresser and having it always available as if she might return unexpectedly. The good that came out of it was that through talking to each other we discovered that we were normal, lonely human beings who had been temporarily stuck in the traffic jam of perpetual grieving. By being with each other we were able to work our way free.

Today that group has joined two other chapters, all united now under the umbrella of a wonderful national organization of bereaved parents called The Compassionate Friends. (National Headquarters, Post Office Box 1347, Oak Brook, Illinois 60521, phone 312/323-5010.)

11
The Making of a Survivor

It became apparent to me presently that I did not know enough about suicide to provide the help needed by some of our clients. I had been studying community counseling at Georgia State University but now my needs were changing. So I applied for graduate work at Emory University, also in Atlanta. Emory did not award a master's degree in suicidology, nor did it have a specific course leading to it. However, through the Graduate Institute of the Liberal Arts (the ILA), I could apply for admission in an interdisciplinary study program in the subject of my choice. I had to prove to the admissions committee that I was self-motivated, that courses existed relating to suicidology, and that I would have the means of using this education in my career.

Returning to my home with an arm full of catalogs, I charted a program of study that included psychology, sociology, and anthropology. The subjects I wanted were available but distributed among various disciplines. I wrote a seven-page application that involved a critical decision: should I or should I not admit that my son had killed himself. Would that fact help or hurt? Knowing the common cultural aversion to suicide, I feared that a frank admission might ruin my application. Yet, I knew there was only one way to go, so I told my story as honestly as I could.

I was accepted and became the only graduate student studying suicidology in the University. The responsibility of choosing my curriculum required faculty supervision, and warm-hearted Professor Fred R. Crawford, of the Department of Sociology and the Director of the Center for Research in Social Change, agreed to become my advisor. Because I was employed full-time and had responsibilities as a wife and mother, it was possible to take only one course each quarter. It was an ideal arrangement. I was elated to be on the Emory campus. I was charting my own future. I knew where I was going and I was indeed launching into the business of making meaning out of meaninglessness.

The anniversary of a suicide is hurtful. So are birthdays but an anniversary usually seems worse. The original is neon-lighted in one's mind, and it often glows through the preceding and following nights and days. My husband and I chose to honor Mitch's death by celebrating its anniversary with a family holiday at a Georgia beach. Being together, though we had been hurt, renewed the realization of how greatly we were blessed, not only by the continuing presence of each member of our family but by the special richness of our years with Mitch. Our vacation-holiday became a time of frequent cleansing tears but also of much happiness.

Soon afterward, I had a mysterious dream. Unlike my earlier "salmon can dream," already reported, in which the details were etched in my mind, this dream was fuzzed and smeared like a painting by DeKooning or Jackson Pollock. It was the first time I had dreamed of Mitch in a year. Throughout, I was conscious of his presence, but his surroundings eluded me. I wondered what that meant.

That morning, I attended a lecture. Richard E. Felder, M.D., a wise and experienced psychotherapist, was the speaker. Among other things he told us of the Senoi people, a tribe in Malaya, who used the subjects of their dreams to help regulate their lives.

As I understood it, adults of the tribe met each morning and told each other their dreams. By common consent, they chose a character about whom some tribesman had dreamed (perhaps a potentate or chieftain) who was deemed powerful enough to dispense favors. It was their daily habit, Dr. Felder said, to ask that dream-actor for a gift.

What was the gift? It had to be one that all of the tribe could use, one that would make their common existence nobler, more comfortable, less painful. And each adult had to settle in his own mind what use he would make of that gift in his day-to-day life.

I was awed by the coincidence. The previous night, I had dreamed of Mitch. Hours later, I was being urged to ask him for a gift. Somehow, I knew that the speaker had become involved in my healing.

That night, I very deliberately followed his instructions. I asked Mitch for a gift—any gift—knowing that whatever he gave me, if anything, would be a treasure. A significant dream followed. I dreamed of a tree of life, and I was that tree, with roots deeply planted in the earth, and a strong trunk leading up to branches that were covered with green leaves. The leaves and branches moved in the wind. They were flexible and moved gracefully, somewhat like a willow tree. The tree was lovely and growing, and I felt good about my tree-self.

Behind the tree, I could make out a beautiful orange sun and a battalion of clouds that reflected a gorgeous sunset. The sun gave warmth and life to the tree, and I was aware that the sun was Mitch, my son. Sun—son. A warming sense of peace filled me.

When I awoke, I continued to feel the same tranquility. I got out of bed and went straight to my closet and retrieved a checkered flannel shirt that had belonged to Mitch and which I had hidden on a top shelf. I had forgotten about it for months. It was the only remaining garment of his that had not been laundered by our efficient housekeeper. It retained his special scent and I had not been able to bring myself to wash it. That shirt was my last real connection with his living. Now I took it from its hiding place and buried my face in it, breathing deeply one last time. I was ready to let it go. I then put it on, took it off, and hung it on a hanger to air and be laundered. Later, I joyfully gave it to one of Mitch's brothers. I had taken one more step in my healing process.

The next night—the second night after Dr. Felder's lecture—I dreamed that the world was coming to an end. It was a time of war and a battle raged. Bombs were falling, soldiers were shooting, and an earthquake was shaking the earth. I had the feeling that I had to reach Richard Bailey, a close friend and advisor, who had contributed greatly to my healing. As we met with the earth trembling under our feet, I asked him for a gift. He said, "My gift to you is a serpent. It is not poisonous. It may bite and cause you pain but you will survive. And the experience will teach you something that you need to know."

I was dismayed. I did not expect a serpent, but I held it in my hands and felt its body twining itself around my arms, and I was strangely unafraid. When I awoke, the details were vivid. Immediately, I felt that there was a profound connection between the two dreams, first of myself as a tree of life warmed by Mitch's sun, and second of the serpent that would hurt but not kill. Inevitably, I recalled the Biblical story of the serpent in the Garden of Eden and the Tree of Life.

On the third night, I dreamed again. This time, it was about my husband, Jack. Again, I asked for a gift. The present he gave me was a magic carpet, and I was surprised and pleased. Toward the end of the dream, I received a revelation concerning its meaning. My husband was giving me his support for whatever role I chose to assume, whether it was as wife, mother, counselor, administrator, or perhaps all of them. At this crucial crossroads of my life, he was telling me through the magic carpet symbol, that I should follow whatever star I might choose.

I awoke with a deep sense of calm. I felt free, supported and loved. The conflict in my subconscious between career and family, hitherto suppressed, had been resolved. I know that my husband's dream gift was what in reality he had already given me. I had only to accept his gift to be at peace.

Three aspects of my life were clarified for me in those three nights of dreaming. Together, they represented, I believe, my womanhood, my profession, and my parenting. I shall not try to analyze them here in psychoanalytic terms, but they added a new dimension to my counseling work. Since then, dream work has become an important part of my own therapy and growth. I still follow Dr. Felder's advice whenever I dream of a person who is near and dear and invariably I either ask for or send that person a symbolic gift.

A persistent component of the process of recovery seems to be the mood swings which persist through the weeks and months of mourning like an endless ride on a rollercoaster. One soars to a euphoric peak on Sunday and then, within the week, dives into a hellish abyss. My yo-yo mood presently reached unanticipated levels. My recovery was complicated by an increasing number of clients coming to the Link and our need for more counseling rooms. Expansion of our facilities became necessary. In concert with our Board of Directors, I asked the community for help. It responded with money and materials. Clients continued to come to our caring and professional staff. This response made me feel useful and hopeful again.

12
The Savage God Returns

From the beginning, counseling has been rewarding. The Link's staff devoted its time to drug abuse, alcoholism, runaways, loneliness, marital discord, and family disruption. I continued to talk occasionally about suicide prevention and the healing of suicide-caused grief. I showed myself as a survivor. In most cases, that seemed to be enough to help others.

One day, a friend and I were walking through a parking lot, chatting and chuckling, when I saw a car trailing us. It abruptly drew ahead, stopped, and a woman I had never seen got out. She approached me, her arms wide. "It's so wonderful to see you smiling," she said, embracing me. "After what you've been through, it gives me hope. Thank you for surviving." Then she returned to her car and drove away.

Similar episodes told me that I had entered a *terra incognito,* a strange territory where the need for consolation and closure of grief was as pressing as even the worst family problem. In time, I began to get referrals from outside the counseling profession. Ministers and lawyers usually made them. They said I would be listened to because I had been there.

Presently, the magic carpet which my husband had given me in my dream became very active indeed. The Compassionate Friends of America, composed of bereaved parents, invited me to address them at a convention in Kansas City. I accepted and told my personal story, assured them they could survive, and urged them to acknowledge their own grief, hiding nothing.

I held a workshop for high school counselors, warning them of the signs that might predict a potential suicide. I conducted seminars in a half-dozen universities and at several conventions. The response to my story was so appreciative that when national magazines quoted me or I appeared on a TV program, I felt that I was making a contribution. It helped me to close the deep wound in my psyche, and it helped others.

A friend warned me to go slow. She pointed out the danger of spreading myself too thin. She said, "Don't crusade or allow your suicide prevention work to become a temple that you are building to your son." I appreciated and needed to hear caution to keep my emotions in balance. And yet, if audiences of professional workers could hear of the experiences of myself and others, this might hinder the destructive growth of teenage suicide. I vowed to proceed carefully.

Then came a call from a small town in Georgia. Within three days, two of their teenage children had killed themselves. Apparently, drugs were involved. The town was terrified. Someone asked a friend in Atlanta for help. He knew of my work and believed I could assist. I was invited to accompany him and an authority on drug abuse prevention to address a mass meeting of citizens. I cancelled all appointments and we were flown to Sommerville in a tiny plane. Twelve hundred people were waiting.

We are both common-sense consultants. He provided down-to-earth recipes for combating the drug epidemic which was believed to be related to the suicides. I tried to soothe roiled emotions by speaking openly about the tragedy of suicide. I spoke of the myths and fears that suicide caused, and the need to understand why it happened. I talked about the process of grief and anger that they might experience. To serve those who were already feeling depressed or self-destructive, I tried to direct them to their local counseling resources. Finally, I encouraged them to face the truth, being honest with themselves and with one another so as to prevent future tragedies.

Already, the students of the high school were in a tumult, one group blaming another, one person another, with many blaming themselves. I knew that suicide epidemics had developed from similar situations. My talk to this community and the following day to 700 students in the high school explained how a wound in one's body healed, its progress slow but usually certain, that when a scar formed it could soon be forgotten. A wound in one's psyche was different, passing through stages of recovery, then regressing to violent infections which might or might not give way to eventual healing. I told them that combating the wound we called grief required understanding and openness and courage. As intimately as I could, I described my progress after Mitch's suicide from the early stages of shock and guilt through anger to eventual acceptance and hope. I said, "You will never be the same but it does get better." I shared with them my feelings that suicide was certainly an option for ending pain and loneliness, but that there were other options that also deserved consideration. Talking to a counselor was one—the local mental health center was providing in-school counseling; hurting students needed only to give themselves permission to seek help. Afterwards, scores of young people came forward to share their feelings and tell me that they were grateful for a frank discussion and a better understanding of the subject.

Finally, I spent some hours with the families of the two children who had died. All were in despair and sick over their own assumed failures. I knew their feelings well.

One of the Sommerville suicides had happened on the night of a basketball game. A mother, suspicious of her daughter's behavior before she left the home, went to her bedroom and found drugs. I was told that she drove her car to the school, dragged the girl from the gym, and took her home and spanked her. That night, the daughter swallowed a lethal dose of pills. When I spoke to her mother, the right or wrong of her act was irrelevant. She sobbed as I held her. She said, "My child's blood is on my hands." As long as I live, I shall never forget her sobbing. We sat in silence as we held each other, for what could words do? The hours passed but her misery would not lessen. She had yet to learn that her disciplinary action had not caused her daughter's death. It was but one in a series of events that led to the decision to die.

When sharing with others in grief, one uses himself as his best resource. When faith and trust in God and one's religion or spiritual beliefs have provided comfort and solace, as it did for me, it is natural to want to prescribe this help for others. It must be remembered, however, that all people do not have a recognized faith. This must be respected, in this author's opinion. Religious beliefs need not be pressed on the nonbeliever. However, it is sometimes helpful to share one's faith. On occasion, the other person will be comforted by your concern and openness, but it should always be presented without proselytizing. I am reminded of my sense of comfort and reassurance provided by the calm presence of three ministers: Rev. Don Harrison, Rev. Joel Hudson, and Rev. Charles Fulghum, during the days following Mitch's death. Their practical and spiritual guidance sustained us.

The family in Sommerville huddled together, praying for forgiveness and for strength and the will to survive.

It was almost dawn when I returned to Atlanta and stumbled into bed.

13
Another Kick in the Stomach

It was during the ensuing week that I sensed the onslaught of a period of depression that frightened me. Looking back through time, I recalled an earlier mood swing only a few months after Mitch's death that had come from nowhere. My husband and the boys and I had attended a hockey game following an earlier family custom. It was our first excursion since Mitch's death. Instead of diversion, I found youth and vitality all about me, thousands of young men bursting with life. My soul rebelled at the injustice. It was unfair that those youths should be happy and exuberant when my son lay dead. I sat through that entire game silently screaming.

The onslaught of depression was usually heralded by signs that I learned early. I recalled my pickiness with others, my sudden, not-to-be-denied outbursts of temper. Before birthdays or holidays, I would feel abandoned and friendless. Usually, care-taking friends recognized the signs also and invited me to lunch and shopping expeditions. On those days, our talk was about both the past and the future. Sometimes I called others and asked for their companionship. We all knew why we had joined in this ceremony. Being together was both comforting and healing.

I know now that I was nursing the beginning of an awareness that suicide was too big an enemy to be destroyed by an educational program or by any one group of persons. To be sure, a few score discouraged youths had been helped, but there remained so many others unreached, and Sommerville was an example. Everywhere, the lines of communication between parents and their children, teachers and children, and peers and children were stretching tighter. The result was isolation, loneliness, runaways, and drug abuse and, often too suicide. Nor was any remedy in sight, not in the school systems, in helping organizations, nor in the plans of mental health agencies. What should I do? What could I do?

I had one more workshop lecture to give at a university in New York City. Famous suicidologists had been invited to speak there. Perhaps they would advance some mind-boggling program. I think I wanted something like Moses bringing the Ten Commandments down from the top of Mount Sinai. Somehow, I thought that such a big problem could be solved by "thinking big."

In New York, I told of my experience and listened to the other speakers. The men and women I met were big guns, movers and shakers, doctors of philosophy, and scholar-physicians. They presented scientific research reports, meticulous surveys, and scholarly papers. Many of the workshops were productive. To the hapless and hopeless youths in my area, they offered little. I went home disheartened.

My son, Bobby, age 18, met me with bad news. "I'm sure glad you're here, Mom. Randy committed suicide."

I could not believe it. Randy was Bobby's classmate and friend, a member of the wrestling team, and a popular boy. We knew him well, or so we thought.

"He shot himself last night," Bobby said. "I'd like for us to go right over to see his folks. They've asked me to be a pallbearer."

We hurried to Randy's home and found his parents in the identical state of shock and confusion that had originally numbed our family. We held each other tightly, silenced by our joint sorrows. As we clasped one another, I saw clearly the Faustian paradox of my recent months of racing around the nation to conduct anti-suicide workshops on distant campuses while the savage god was spreading his deadly poison in my own backyard.

Critical of myself for neglecting my own community, I wanted to know the details of this newest tragedy. Randy had gone to a party and on the way home had damaged his car. His father heard his explanation and said, "Don't worry about it. We'll work it out." It was no big deal.

Next morning, Randy was missing. Unexplained blood stains soiled his bedsheets. Neighbors formed a posse to search the area. His body lay in a vacant lot behind a nearby school where he had shot himself. The easy explanation was that he had damaged his automobile, been unable to face up to the consequences, and so had killed himself. It was a classic case with a classic conclusion, and I knew the conclusion was wrong. The mishap had merely triggered the final act. Randy's troubles, like Mitch's, lay buried in the past. They had accumulated over a time span that included many, many victories and defeats, and when the defeats seriously outnumbered the victories, his pain intensified. And finally, it was more than he could bear. I know that pain, I know its bitter taste in the back of the throat and its sound in the inner ear. Luckily, for me, good friends and good therapy subdued it.

That afternoon, we attended Randy's funeral and I felt the gnawing pain of grief again. Hundreds of his schoolmates moved through the trees in the same cemetery in which my Mitch lay buried. As tears flowed from a thousand eyes, I embraced dozens of children in a vain effort to assuage their hurt. Some were shedding sorry tears but others had angry tears, for which they punished themselves by feeling guilty.

The school principal, an old acquaintance, stood near the grave, white-faced and distrait. Remembering my encounter with the students in Sommersville, I told him I would be glad to speak to his students about grief and mourning if he thought it would be appropriate. He accepted my offer. When I asked Bobby for his approval, he said, "If it will help anybody, please do it."

Next day, I did. Six hundred students had gathered in the high school auditorium. Attendance was voluntary because this was an unscheduled meeting; the standard curriculum had not included a memorial for a suicide.

It was Sommersville all over again. Many students felt guilty and were angry with themselves for feeling guilty. "How can I be angry at a dead friend? But I am," exclaimed a 15-year-old boy.

I had learned that kids were turning their anger toward God, their friends, their teachers, and their parents. Some spoke of wanting to end their own lives in this unfair world. I spoke calmly, touching on all that I had learned about the shock of suicide and recovery from the terrible pain it caused. Earlier, my Mitch had gone to that same high school. Earlier, he and his jazz ensemble had played their music from this same stage. I spoke to the kids as if they were adults. I told them that guilt was natural and anger was natural, indeed necessary. I told them that the worst thing that could happen now was that they might hide from themselves.

"So talk about Randy," I urged. "Talk to each other and to your parents. Some of you may want to cling to your guilt until it turns to hate. If you do, it will deform you. I have a thing about guilt. I say, if you feel guilty, *feel guilty*. Get into it. Feel it until you're tired of it. If you feel mad, *feel mad*. If you feel sad, *feel sad*. I mean, get into it hard. And do it all with no self-judgment, no self-blame." They listened intently.

"If you feel guilt, it's because you are normal and human. But if you choose to hold onto that feeling forever you may need to ask yourself why you need to stay there. Are you punishing yourself for something that's real? Sometimes it feels like you're saying, 'If I don't feel rotten, it's like I'm betraying Randy's memory.' But by hanging onto your self-punishment, you may turn mourning into a life style that can produce a twisted human being."

I urged, "Most of all, don't deny your feelings. What you deny acquires enormous power over your life. Those things that you push back into your mind, like the word suicide, for instance, pile up inside you, and when the pile is big enough it may explode.

"I believe that the things you don't deal with openly will fester and swell until they acquire enough power to control your life.

"The point is that if you feel something, even if it's negative, lay it out on the table, and look at it. Then you may eventually get tired of it. And then you can let it go.

"It's natural to agonize over Randy's death," I concluded, "but don't stay silent. Talk about the crazy things he did, the good things, the bad things. He was a human being like yourselves, trying to find himself. Yesterday, we buried him in Arlington Cemetery, but don't you bury him in the back of your minds.

Keep him up front because he was a part of your life and a part of your learning experience in this high school. So honor him by speaking his name."

I talked for thirty minutes. It was a profound experience for me. It was also a difficult experience, because Mitch's face was often before me as I spoke. But tomorrow would be easier, I knew, because I had completed a cycle. I was no longer depressed. I stood before these kids, vulnerable in sharing my own painful loss of my son, but bearing witness to the ability of the human psyche to survive.

14
You Can Make a Difference

Life goes on and months have passed since Randy's funeral, and I ask myself what I have learned about this jungle where any crossroads can lead to a dead child's body. Well, I have learned that I can never stop a suicide on my own. The matrix of a victim's life contains thousands of contact points which have either inflamed or soothed his ego. He alone can count his scars, his open wounds. The best I can offer is a willingness to listen and a shoulder on which to cry. And when I have heard his story, I can only suggest options.

A Johnny-come-lately, I am a tardy addition to a long line of would-be care-givers who have been shocked into a new and perplexing role. Our single-minded objective has been intended to stop the self-slaughter of our youth. Thus far, our results are picayune. We can meet a victim one-on-one and offer pro-life arguments, we can use every delaying tactic in the kit bag, but the choice for life must be made by the other person. One loses or one wins, and I still do not know why. Sometimes, it seems to me that the merest offer of one's love and understanding—the bare fact that we are listening—is enough to tilt the decision toward life. On the contrary, some individuals will reject every offer of rescue.

Organized attempts at deliverance are a fairly recent development. An American Baptist minister, the Rev. Harry Watson, was one of the first to muster an army of volunteers into a suicide prevention movement. He called it the Save-A-Life League. Its function was to supply a friendly advisor to any person who called for help. Later, a British divine, the Rev. Chad Varsh, saw that suicidal death was becoming a cult fad among fashionable youth in England and he assembled a similar posse which he named the Samaritans. Today, Samaritan chapters are doing good work throughout the British Commonwealth. They dispense no drugs, no soothing syrups, no psychological fixes. Their only medicine is friendship, immediate and nonjudgmental. Not surprisingly, it often works.

Uncle Sam was late in coming into the battle. In 1958, our Federal government backed a group of scientists and researchers in California who founded the now famous Suicide Center of Los Angeles. This group theorized, experimented, and currently produces a variety of programs. Today, scores of similar centers exist as well as 300 or so suicide "hot lines" which are served day and night by counselors who wait beside their telephones.

Of two things we can be reasonably certain. First, most experts assure us that the urge to commit suicide usually lasts for only a brief time, from a month, a week, a day or so, to a span of minutes only. Second, threats of killing one's self are usually a cry for help. It follows that the "hot-line" and the delay it encourages is probably one of the best antidotes for most youthful death wishes.

The search for a panacea has spread now around the world to include sociologists, psychologists, psychiatrists, physicists, physicians, and pharmacologists. The bottom line is that we are still scratching the surface. Headlines continue to announce boomlets of suicidal behavior. Statistics continue to place the rate in our own United States about midway between the best and the worst of international record keepers. Nor is improvement seriously anticipated.

As I face the future, as a mother and counselor, I am aware that our nation fights other social afflictions with only meager success. We fight the drug traffic and drugs abound. We fight alcoholism but drunkenness continues. We fight wife-beating and child abuse but violence rages on. We fight criminal rape but defilement persists. Some aspects of life seem to be immutable, as are birth and death. Perhaps suicide is immutable, too.

For every completed suicide, there are dozens that are uncompleted. Regardless of whether or not death supervenes, the social stigma comes with the attempt, and its disgrace may stain a family or perhaps a community. This is not because we still believe that vengeful ghosts return to punish our misdeeds, as of yore, but because we sophisticated moderns have developed an irresistible need to place blame. Placing blame apparently restores bruised egos and absolves guilt. Thus, life can go on. But sometimes not for those who are blamed. They may be stigmatized. Often they bear the brunt of neighborhood gossip. Temporarily, many become emotionally crippled. Their road to recovery is difficult.

Among these thousands who are innocently injured, there is a great searching for a mode of survival. The quest is common to spouses, mothers, fathers, brothers, sisters, teachers, preachers, athletic coaches, and pals. It is not surprising that they hide from sight, that they fight back their memories and even the names of those they have loved and lost. As the saying goes, they all have been "there," *in extremis*, and they want desperately to understand why. Or at the very least, to understand why they can never understand.

Many things have changed since I addressed that spooked student body in Atlanta on the day after Randy's funeral. I know little of what has happened since to those young people. But I am certain of two consequences which are significant to me.

First, over the intervening months, many of them have stopped me on the street, dropped into my home to talk, or sent me notes. They all said the same things, of which this paragraph from a young girl's letter is typical.

"I was a close friend of Randy's," she wrote. "I was hurting so bad that day when you came to our school that I was on the verge of trying to follow him. Your common-sense talk gave me hope. If you survived, I guess I can too. I now have the courage to talk about it and to face it. I am grateful."

Second, the depression that had paralyzed me finally lifted out of my mind and gave my spirit permission to take charge of my life.

Much thought has brought me to the conclusion that the act

of suicide is similar, in one way, to that of a stone tossed into a lake. It makes a splash, either small or large, but then it sinks. Always, it sends ripples in all directions, in a concentric washing of every leaf, chip, and waterbug afloat. Though the stone itself has vanished, its impact steadily widens to embrace unknown distant areas.

So it is with those of us who have survived a suicide. Startled, tossed about, thrust toward our own extinction, we have no choice but to ride the dizzying waves. So I perceive a role for this survivor and for many other survivors. To be with others in their pain, I feel, is not an unworthy goal.

This is not to say that one must surrender to the savage god. It is to say, however, that there is always more to any act of violence than the fate that overtakes its perpetrator. Living through the period since my son's death has clarified that fact again and again.

Very clearly, we survivors are an endangered species.

A goodly number of survivors have become my clients and my friends, and there will be others. So where do we go from here?

I am sobered by this fact: the problem began with the beginning of time, and it is not likely to go away. The church had a go at it and failed. The state had a go at it and failed. Science had a go at it and failed. I had a go at it and failed.

For me, the issue is clear. We cannot exterminate the savage god but we can abate his vileness. The means and the methods, as I have learned, are in our own hands. They include open talk, a candid facing of the reality of our being deserted, confessing both the good and the bad points of our departed loved ones, building no shrines but honoring the happy days and deeds that once brightened our lives, sharing the lessons we have learned, allowing our guilt to turn to regret, and finally, without forgetting, simply letting go.

I no longer feel despair. We who survive may not be able to change the world but surely we can make a difference.

PART TWO:
BLUEPRINT FOR RENEWAL

15

Sorrow Knows No Strangers

The ringing of the telephone broke the silence of a spring morning. My peaceful dream shattered, I tried to orient myself. Where was I? Where's the phone? "Hello! Who? Oh, Bruce Pemberton? Yes, I can hear you...."

An old friend and clinical psychologist was calling to ask a favor. My joy at hearing his voice was short-lived. I heard him say, "I've been up all night with dear friends. Their 18-year-old daughter has committed suicide. She shot herself yesterday. Would you be willing to talk to the mother on the phone? I think you can help her since you've lived through the same thing."

Now I was awake! "The same thing," he'd said. The shock of those words catapulted me into the past. Three years had passed since I faced the horror and agony of my own son's suicide.

I remembered the shock of it. I recalled the confusion of disbelief, the contradiction of my denial and the immutable truth. I had wanted to bargain with God, with fate, with destiny . . . to undo . . . to make it not so. I recalled my feeling of self-obliterating guilt. What had I done—or not done? How had I failed as a mother? How could I go on living?

I had even felt anger at my dead son for wasting his precious life. But in the same breath, I was ashamed of myself; how could I be angry with my own dead child? I could and I was. But guilt enveloped me. In the weeks that followed, I was to learn that expressing this anger was an important part of my healing.

Slowly I discovered substance and meaning again. I came to realize that life is tenuous for everyone, and that though one's fate is unknown with respect to the future, one still has today. Today is now, within grasp of mind and body, as you live it. You may not be master of your fate, but you can be master of your Now. Waste it or cherish it, which shall it be? The choice is yours.

I was at the end of a waiting telephone line. Another mother was in distress, and I was being asked to help. Three years earlier, I would not have known what to say. I wondered, did I know enough even after so many months of study and counseling and therapy? I braced myself against the challenge. She was a stranger, and yet she was not.

Bruce's voice was making an introduction. I heard myself saying, "Hello, Cathy. I'm so sorry. I know it's unbearable ... it's unfair. I guess the main thing I'd like to say to you right now is something you may not believe. Very simply, it is this: You can survive! I know your pain because I've lived it, and someday it will lessen and you *will* be able to go on with your life." I thought she might not hear me and I pressed my lips to the mouthpiece. "Cathy, my own son died the same way as your daughter. But I've made it. My husband has made it. My other three sons have made it. And you can, too."

Silence held us together.

My awkward monologue continued: "Cathy, you're probably still dazed and in shock. As you begin to know what's going on inside you, understand that whatever you are feeling, is natural and normal. When it happened to me, I was helped by letting my feelings out and refusing to bottle them up. At times, I thought I was going crazy, and you may, too. This fear is normal; it's a part of recovering from our helplessness. How I wish I'd known then that I was reacting just like so many other bereaved parents."

More silence.

Words tumbled out as I tried to fill the void ... to soften the blow. "Lots of people will tell you how you should feel and what to do. In these next days, please know that you alone can decide what is best for you, what is right for you. So make your choices for your own sake, not for anyone else. Ask for what you want. Insist on it. Here's one other thought: You must save your strength right now, so let your family and your close friends take care of you. Your doing so will help them and it will help you, too."

"Okay," was the weak reply. Cathy was listening.

"It may be helpful to know that no one thing caused it. I added. "You may want to blame yourself and...."

She interrupted harshly. "But why? Why did Julie do this? I don't understand why. We knew she was depressed and had stopped eating. Her weight was down to 80 pounds. But we thought she was getting better. Why did she have to do it? Why, why, why?"

I took a deep breath. "I can't tell you why. I wish I could. But I'm glad you're asking that question because it's important to ask." This mother needed to find her own answers—every survivor does—to discover for herself that there are many reasons and there are none. Probably she would never know why, but she needed to try to find out so she could satisfy her hunger to know. Eventually, she would be able to let go of her unanswerable questions. Now, however, she needed something to hang onto.

"I don't think either of our children really wanted to die," I said. "I believe it was the overwhelming pain in their lives that drove them to it. Perhaps they couldn't stand the pain of living as they perceived it."

"Maybe that's it, Iris."

Was it too soon, I wondered, to tell her that we parents can only give our children our humaness, which means our positive qualities along with our negative qualities? Should I try to explain that what a child does with our parenting is his own choice? His life is his responsibility. Was it too soon to say that we are a part of his family and therefore we are a part of his living and dying. Unless there is malicious intent, we must forgive ourselves for whatever part we played in this tragedy. I would wait, I decided. Impulsively, I said, "Cathy, would it be helpful if I came over?"

"Oh, yes! I'd like that."

"I'll see you in a little while."

As I lowered the receiver, I was enveloped by the same sensation I had first felt years earlier. It has been said, "The loss of one's own child is profound and devastating. It is one of the worst blows a person can experience." But it is also painful to witness, if only because we are so impotent in trying to help.

I was impotent all right, but I shared in memory Cathy's isolation and aloneness. A suicide is an unthinkable offense in today's polite society. Its stigma cuts one off from reality, as well as from one's normal recuperative resources. Somehow I hoped to deposit in her mind some of the truths I had learned over months of personal struggle.

But first, I thought, she needed to be held. No other symbol of concern means so much. In the meantime, I was due at my office. My appointments would have to be reshuffled. I telephoned that I would be in later. (I little dreamed how late it would be.) Cathy's urgent needs filled my mind. I could not be certain of my welcome. Had I invited myself into her home? Her family might reject me or throw me out. She had mentioned a husband and three other children. Did I have anything to offer? I wasn't certain, but I would go.

Preparing for my drive to her home, I recalled the crippling blows under which I had bowed, and the long, slow miracle through which I and my husband and my three surviving sons had come to terms with our loss. Perhaps before this tragic day was finished, I could pass a piece of that miracle on to Cathy.

A pad and pencil lay on the kitchen table. Suddenly, I sat down and began to write: words, then phrases, finally sentences. My feelings begat thoughts that begat guidances; the ups and downs of my healing. Might I fashion a life preserver, I wondered, composed of words to which Cathy and her family could cling?

"The suicide of a child is one of the worst things that can happen to a parent," I wrote. "I know because my own son committed suicide. But you will survive it if you choose to. I know you can. Your mind may be filled for days with doubt, but you can survive. Then you will know your own strength, and you will be able to survive anything."

She had wanted to know why. All parents want to know why.

The question cuts more deeply than any other. I would remind Cathy of our talk. "Keep asking for an answer," I urged. "I suspect that no definitive answer will ever be granted, but you need to struggle with it. The struggle, I've learned, is more important than the reason why. After a time, you can let it go and not need to know anymore."

Guilt is another paralyzing emotion that often envelops survivors. It batters the ego as nothing else in the world. It scuttles the will to live. It parades a stream of bitter memories across the screen of your mind. Guilt often comes from the sorrow of not being able to keep a loved one from pain or from suicide. "Expect to feel guilt. Expect it to be hard to handle," I continued writing. "You will ask—what did I fail to do? What did I do wrong? Ultimately, you must save yourself by fixing in your mind the truth that you gave to your child your very best. You gave the gift of yourself and your humanness. So ask also: What did she do with your gifts? Her actions were totally her responsibility. So what did she do? Understand this and one day you can let go of your guilty feeling. When that happens, you are one step closer to acceptance and peace of mind. On the other hand some persons feel no guilt at all, being reassured by their consciousness of having done all they could."

During my own pain, a friend had warned me about sorrow's other face, the one that is ugly and vindictive. Its lips snarl and attack one's "cool." It is called anger. I wanted to tell Cathy about what I had learned of the cleansing power of anger.

"One of these days, you will almost certainly feel a kind of rage," I wrote. "Most people do. Impossible, you think. How can a parent be angry with her dearest possession? It happens. Many experts say it *should* happen. They feel that it flushes and purges and sweetens the mind. It allows the tie to be broken. In my case, it struck me belatedly, but when it hit, it was horrid. I went to my son's grave one afternoon and demanded of the air and the sky and God himself that they tell me what right my son had to leave me in such great pain, to defile my life, to have refused my efforts to help. Finally, my anger burned itself out. It was over, like a plunge across an icy pool. If you do not feel anger, know that it may not be necessary for you. There is no absolute formula for healing."

What else could I say? I would be with her only a short time. I recalled her tight-throated responses on the phone, like whispers flung through a locked door. My own relief, I recalled, had come through talk and more talk. Many mothers have used that escape hatch.

"You may need to talk about your loss. Talk to your husband and your children. This is natural and it is healing. I even found myself talking to my tailor and my grocer about what happened. Talk about the good times and the not-so-good times. Tell the story until you're finished telling it." It sounded preachy, I thought, "but talk to your friends, too. Close friends especially. Allow your family and friends to take care of you," I said. "You are not required to be strong now. Cry if you feel like it. Cry wherever you are. It is natural and healing. Grief is not something you can bottle up and screw on the cap. That way guarantees future pain and disaster. Instead, throw the cap away, and one day your bottle of pain will be emptied and you may know peace. You will never be the same, you will be different, but you can know joy again. If you honestly feel no need to talk about your loss, accept that as right for you. Do what is comfortable for you."

It was almost time to go to Cathy's. I took my paragraphs to the typewriter and ran off several carbons, adding: "Talk and keep talking . . . about your child and your life together . . . of the good times and the bad. Know that others will grieve differently, particularly family members. Respect their way. Allow yourself to cry and release your feelings. Most of all, know that you can survive."

A worry entered my mind. Cathy and I had never met. Would she think I was presumptuous? I was warmed suddenly by a valedictory sentence that flowed from my flying fingers, without warning, without embarrassment. Perhaps it would help. I titled the paper with these words: "Though We Meet as Strangers, By Our Love We Shall Be Known."

My clock chimed, telling me to go to Cathy.

16
A Time for Holding

I found Cathy Talone's house* after a thirty-minute drive to her downtown Atlanta neighborhood, A row of white frame residences lined the street. I mounted the steps, crossed a large porch, rang the bell and waited. Hearing no response, I knocked. Through the glass door I could see a darkened and deserted living room. Perhaps this is the wrong place, I thought. Standing awkwardly before the door, I was beginning to regret that I had come. Even if I were admitted, I knew that I could say little to ease Cathy's agony. Then I remembered that it was never words alone that comforted. It was simply being with the person. Again, I rang the bell.

A woman opened the door and looked at me with tired eyes. "I'm Iris," I said. "I believe Cathy is expecting me."

"She's having a rough time," she said. "You can follow me." We went through the living room, down a hallway, and into a bedroom. Almost apologetically my guide said, "Cathy's in bed. She didn't sleep all night."

The room was shadowed by full-length drapes drawn together to block the sunlight. Cathy had pulled the covers up over her

---

*The family name used here, Talone, is fictitious. It has been adopted in order to protect the privacy of this generous family of survivors.

head. As I sat on the bed, I said, "Cathy, this is Iris. I'm here." I leaned down and put my arms around the faceless form under the sheet and held her close. Gradually, I felt her rigidity soften as her sobs diminished. But she didn't speak, not then, not for another hour.

The other woman had found a place behind me on the bed and after a time she said, "I'm Sarah, a friend of Cathy's. My daughter died two years ago in an auto accident, so I sort of know what Cathy's going through."

"Oh, I'm sure you do," I said, turning toward her. Tears flooded her eyes as she reached for tissues at the end of the bed. Moving closer, she rested her head on my shoulder. Moments before, we were total strangers. Now, our destinies joined, we sat holding one another united by ties of maternal sorrow. Losing a child is not the right order of things. One expects to bury one's parents, but not one's children. It's all wrong . . . backwards! Accidents are hard enough to understand, but what malice is it that infects so many of our youth that they willfully end their lives?

For an hour, we three held each other. Sarah and I shared phrases such as, "It's okay—go ahead and get it out. You need to let go." After a while, Cathy was able to vent her anguish, even losing control so completely that she no longer cared how she behaved or how she sounded, not caring about anything. Racking sobs shook her slender body. On some level, I think she knew that her soul's cry was being heard.

Gradually, she became calm and lay still. I remembered that I had not seen her face. It mattered little. We had shared with one another at life's deepest level. It was an hour I shall never forget.

When Cathy first sat up in bed and dropped her sheet, it was to worry about how she looked. Ruefully, she apologized and we all chuckled together. "Thank you for coming. Thank you for being here," she whispered. A lovely, blonde girl slipped into the room and sat beside her mother. I was about to meet Cathy's 15-year-old daughter. "Cindy, this is Iris," her mother said. "Her son died like Julie did and she's come to be with us."

Cindy was polite. "I'm glad to meet you." She quickly turned her attention to her mother. "Mom, are you okay?"

"Yes, I'm okay. I think I'm going to be all right. The doctor gave me something to relax me and I guess I lost control before it took effect."

I thought to myself how easy it is to give a pill to numb the patient and the pain, even though that may not be what is needed. I thought how fortunate it is for Cathy that she had been able to "explode" before succumbing to the anesthetic drug. Sometimes medication is necessary, of course, but how glad I was that grief education is becoming a priority in some medical schools, nursing schools, seminaries, and colleges. I remembered bereaved mothers who were so heavily sedated that they could hardly remember the cause of their mourning. Normal grief is not an emotional illness. It is a process that must be experienced. Sorrow must be accepted and allowed to mature and then, hopefully, be laid aside.

I was suddenly aware that my back ached from the prolonged sitting and the intensity of our emotions. I got up stiffly, said I'd return in a moment, and walked into the hall. A tall man lurched into the passageway. His fist held a crumpled sheet of paper and his cheeks, I noted, were wet. Thus, I met Bill Talone, Cathy's husband of seven years and the devoted stepfather of her four children. Julie had been the second child, age 18. Sam was 20, Cindy 15, and Matt 12. This sensitive man had been a father to Julie since her eleventh birthday. Her suicide had left him devastated.

Struggling to keep his balance, he steadied himself against a wall, looking as if he had been kicked in the stomach. As I approached, he stood doubled over in pain. "It's just not true!" he blurted. "How could she accuse me?" Then he put his arms on my shoulders and sobbed, his knees sagging as I embraced him. Sorrow knows no strangers, I thought. When a moment had passed, he spoke again explaining wildly, "I just found a suicide note Julie wrote me and it's awful. She blames me. She *blames* me! But she's wrong. I'll destroy the note. I'll not let anyone see it."

"You must have loved her very much," I said.

Bill's sobs racked his body again, then a trace of anger began to surface, giving him the energy to reinforce his denial. "You bet I loved Julie," he said. "But her death is not my fault. I loved her. If the others read what she wrote, they'll all hate me. What should I do?"

Experience had taught me that the only way to face the horror of suicide was to face it. To destroy the note or to deny its contents might ultimately add to its destructive power. To read it, sharing it openly with the family, and talking about it together could be the best hope for defusing it.

Matter-of-factly, I said, "That's a tough decision to handle alone. It might help to get another opinion on what Julie really meant in the note."

He thrust the paper into my hand as though he needed someone else, even preferred a stranger, to affirm or deny his fears. "Don't let anybody see it," he demanded, steering me into a small den and retreating to the hall.

I read Julie's message. She seemed to be making a desperate effort to reach a final understanding, impressing on him how she had felt hurt by his fatherly discipline. I had read many similar notes. Some of those who commit suicide must place the blame on others as a way of absolving themselves. In their anger and hostility they will blame loved ones, fate, the world, and circumstances. Wanting to live, as well as wanting to die to relieve the pain, it seemed that the remnants of their demolished ego forced them to blame whatever target was handy. "You have caused me much, much pain," Julie had told her stepfather. "Now, I hope you know how much pain I've been suffering."

I walked into the hall where Bill was pacing. "It's a terrible note to receive," I told him, "but maybe Julie was trying to say more about herself than about you. She was obviously very confused and angry. Maybe your kids might see it that way, too."

He had asked me what to do so I continued. "I have learned that the things I face and don't hide are the things I can eventually let go of. It's the things I deny and refuse to look at that become destructive later on. I suggest that you consider showing the note to your wife, not for her sake, but for your own. It might be very important someday to know that you have hidden nothing from her."

He walked away in silence. I rejoined Cathy. She was sitting up now with her daughter beside her. Sarah had left to attend other visitors. Cathy moved to the center of the bed, making a place for me.

"Has anyone told you what happened to Julie?" she asked.

17
First Aid for Survivors

"I guess it was yesterday . . . it seems a long time ago. Yes, it was Tuesday. Julie had moved next door temporarily to stay with a friend. She was angry with me because I'd kept her home from college. But something strange had happened to her; her weight had dropped to 80 pounds from 120. We couldn't get her to eat. She'd run away for a while and then come back. We finally agreed she could live next door. Our relationship was strained, but I thought she was getting better. We'd had a couple of good talks and she had even begun to accept counseling.

"All day Tuesday, I kept thinking about her, not for any special reason, but she was just on my mind. Our neighbor called to say he had left her asleep and she would be home for dinner. He said she sounded fine. When he got home after work, the front door was locked. He got in a back door and found her lying on her bed. She had shot herself with a handgun.

"When I came home from work, I saw police cars and lots of people around the house next door. Right away, I knew something bad had happened." Fresh tears glistened in Cathy's eyes, spilling down her cheeks. Her body rocked forward and backward like a child in pain. When she regained control, she asked, almost like an immigrant on a strange shore, "Oh God, Iris, what do we do now? What did you do?"

I told her that every bereaved person's experience is different. But there were actions and ideas that had helped my family.

"I'd like to hear them," she said.

"After our talk on the phone this morning," I said, "I typed out a page of things that might help." The folded sheet was in my purse and I handed it to her. "You needn't read it now. Let me tell you about what I wrote."*

"Fine."

I did not know then that my written words were to become her constant companion for the next few days. Later, she told me that she had read and reread them. Sarah reported that all through the following night she had clutched the paper as if it were her only key to survival.

My intention of speaking to her forthrightly was interrupted by her husband, and a handsome young stranger. The newcomer was Sam, the 20-year-old son. Behind him came another son, 12-year-old Matt.

"Well, the whole family's here," Cathy said after introductions. "I've just asked Iris to tell us what we should do next. She's been through it in her own family. She's here to help."

I decided that the time was right for me to share with this stunned family whatever good news I could muster. "The day my son died," I said, "a good friend named Leonard Maholick, who is also a respected Atlanta psychiatrist, came to my home and told my husband and me that he wanted to leave two important thoughts with us. He said the first was that we had a unique opportunity to use the next few days to bring our dazed and disoriented family closer together, if we would. Closer than ever before, he emphasized. A chance to build a bond like nothing else could ever do. We could accomplish this by making a point of always calling a family conference for the airing of all opinions, prior to deciding any important question. 'Children of almost any age are apt to be frightened by closed doors,' he said. 'They feel guilt, often more than parents, and they can be dismayed by being shut out. If you use this opportunity wisely, you can survive and be stronger than ever.' "

---

*Please see Appendix B for a revised summary of the contents of this communication.

Len Maholick's second point had been a semi-theological concept, and I hesitated to present it. But it had meant much to me. Julie's mother might accept it on faith, I thought, but perhaps not her father, with his man-of-the-world practicality. Anyhow, I would try.

"That very first afternoon," I continued, "our friend also told us, 'There is a gift for you in your son's death. You may not believe it at this bitter moment, but it is authentic and it can be yours if you are willing to search for it. To other eyes, it may remain hidden. It won't jump out at you or thrust itself into your life. But your dead son's gift is real and you can find it if you choose.'"

The Talone family looked at me, their eyes round with astonishment. Cathy's face showed puzzlement and Bill's lips made a harsh line. He demanded, "You mean there's something good that can come out of this mess? You mean Julie's killing herself is some kind of crazy gift to Cathy or me? I don't believe it." His voice quivered.

"Bill, it's not that her death is like a going-away present, all boxed and gift-wrapped. Her gift is within you and you will find it only when you decide what to do with this experience." I recalled that my friend's initial suggestion, that Mitch had presented me with a gift, had made me feel as if a protective umbrella had gone up over my head. Suddenly, I knew that I might find meaning and purpose in my knotted agony.

"It was hard for me, too. I share it with you as a hope to hang onto. I mean, I'm here right now only because of my son's suicide. His act directed me into a line of work I'd never even dreamed of before. I had to work hard to discover his gift, but here I am with the privilege of knowing you and being with you in your grief. That's a real gift to me and in turn, it helps me with my own healing process. And I am thankful for that."

I knew I was saying it poorly, but they were silent so I went on. "Here are some other thoughts—during these days of agony, ask for whatever you want and need. If it's something that seems outrageous, ask anyhow. There's no right or wrong at a time like this. Another thing—you'll be having all kinds of strange ideas and feelings. Everyone does. It's normal.

"Many loving people who want to help will be giving you advice about what to do. Some will say snap out of it; some will urge you to take it easy; some will say it's God's will. At a time like this, everybody becomes an instant expert. But you do what *you* want to do. You do what feels right for you. Even if nobody else approves and you still decide for it, *you do it.*"

They were all listening, identifying themselves with the possibilities of their new roles. I added more details: "Face everything about this death as openly as you can. The parts you deny today, you may have to deal with years later. I mean acknowledge that Julie committed suicide. Too many families try to hide the truth. Go down to the funeral home, see Julie, and say goodbye to her. You can't deny her death, so thank her for the good things in her life. All together, you must decide about cremation or not, choosing a casket, buying a burial plot. Do it together. You may not be sure of just what you think or want. The best way to find out is to talk about it. Hang in there together and you're bound to survive."

For another hour, the Talones and I talked about Julie and the events leading to her death. We listed decisions that each of them had to make individually and as a group. By the time the minister came to plan the funeral, they were united by their quiet sharing and by their respect for each other. It was a positive beginning.

Later, I learned from them that Bill had given Julie's suicide note to Cathy. Together, they decided to share it with the children. All of them, I was told, rallied around their stepfather and supported him. A second suicide note had also been found that placed the blame on one of Julie's brothers. Again, her vindictive, confused thoughts were defused by talking about the pain that might have caused such a note to be written.

I left the Talone house as the family prepared to go to the funeral home. They had carefully placed Julie's burial clothes, a favorite shirt, and a faded pair of jeans in a brown paper bag. Already I sensed that they were moving into their next stage of grief.

18
Requiem for a Lost Lady

When I awoke on Friday morning, I remembered that I had made two important commitments. I had promised to attend Julie's funeral, and I had promised to speak about suicide and what I had learned about handling the grief it causes.

Suddenly, I was terror-stricken. I had never spoken at a funeral. The Talones had grasped the straws of my experience so eagerly that I was flattered and accepted their invitation. We had separated after midnight and I tossed restlessly for hours.

I had always assumed that a funeral service was the exclusive business of ministers. Who could know about the hereafter except men of God? In recent years, some youngsters had begun to write their own wedding ceremonies, but I had never heard of a lay person sharing in a funeral. Julie's minister would be a Unitarian, someone had said. That bothered me because I did not know what Unitarians believed about life and death. Nor could the Talones help because they had never met their minister.

I wondered what kind of service a stranger could conduct. A fragment from a long forgotten notebook drifted through my mind. It said that funerals were a universal custom in every culture and that its principal function was not the disposal of a dead body, but to afford psychological support to the bereaved. Today, I believe that.

I had not known Julie either, but I had found some poems she wrote during her final, desperate months. Apparently, writing had been a release from her pain because her jottings covered a hundred scraps of paper. When I read her poetry, as I had read the poetry of my dead son earlier, I realized that I knew a great deal about her. Why, then, should I not speak for her? Why not speak for every hurting youth in a way that could remind listeners of the nearly unbearable stresses that our modern culture imposes? Indeed, why not make this service for our dead Julie a service also for the living?

The funeral chapel in downtown Atlanta was large, airy, and without gloom. Its off-white interior was lighted by high, luminous windows. I was directed to a salon where the family awaited the unfolding of their next episode of grieving. Cathy, Bill and I embraced and clung to each other for a long moment. A bustling funeral director told me that I would find the minister in a small room behind the platform. "He would like to know what you are going to say," he added.

I was puzzled by his tone. It might have indicated regret that a mere lay person was participating in his tidy service. I went at once to the minister's waiting room. Young men in dark suits and muted ties had begun to escort the Talones to their chairs in an alcove off the auditorium. The Reverend Moore was a happy surprise. He knew exactly why he was there and what he was supposed to do.

"I'll open with a few general remarks about death and follow with some suitable readings," he said. "You can deliver your message next, briefly, I trust. I'll close the service. It won't take long. By the way, can you tell me what you intend to say?"

As I outlined my thoughts for him, I heard the soft chords of a guitar playing melodies that Julie had loved. The funeral director interrupted, took our elbows, and led us to the hallway where he stationed each of us opposite a closed doorway leading to the platform. Inhaling noisily, he glanced at his wristwatch and abruptly motioned for us to open our doors and make our entrance.

As I stepped onto the rostrum, my heart leaped with thankfulness. The chapel was alive with sunlike light. Every seat was taken. The platform was walled about by banks of blossoms. The coffin, always a painful sight, was at the center. Two lecterns, one for each of us, had been placed a comfortable distance from the first row of seats. Twin chairs awaited us. As we took our seats, the guitar music softened and faded. After a moment, the Reverend Mr. Moore went to his lectern and began to speak in a calm and reassuring voice.

To this day, I haven't the slightest idea of what he said. In turn, as I walked to the lectern, thoughts drifted through my mind like falling leaves, each labeled with an episode of my own grieving experience. Wind-blown, they would vanish into crannies from which my workaday brain tried to snatch them so they might be filed in some sensible order. My efforts failed and the leaves fell faster.

What subject should I present first to this audience, I wondered. Other questions followed, challenging my presence in this funeral service, asking, "Are you really qualified for this moment?" and "Who appointed you to bring suicide out of the closet?"

A mental door opened and I was suddenly back in the week that followed my son's suicide. Again, I heard familiar voices saying, "Poor dear, she's having a rough time," "Here, son, take care of your mother," and "We'll choose the casket, you don't have to go through that." Men's voices, women's voices, caring voices, wanting to protect me. I suddenly tasted the moment of my rebellion. I had resented being protected. I wanted to participate. Surely I had the right to help bury my own child. I had birthed him, and I would bury him. Eventually, it was I who closed his casket. And it was I who dropped the last handful of red Georgia clay into his grave.

What did the pale and silent Cathy Talone want for herself and her family as she sat in her private alcove? Feminine instinct told me she would always love her dead Julie, but it was hard to love the act of suicide. Julie had been other things as well. She had spent a lifetime performing the endearing chores of childhood, learning the lessons of adolescent give-and-take, and experiencing the passions of young maturity. Most of those years had been beautiful.

Like all of us, Julie had dreamed and fantasized and frequently fallen short. But she had absorbed some of life's deepest virtues and had tried valorously to incorporate them permanently into herself. Idealism is hard to understand in one who puts a gun to her head, but I knew it was there.

Call it self-fulfillment, call it hunger for the fruition of her talents, call it what you will, but she had been an earnest searcher. I held the proof in my hand in one of the poems she had written and left on a torn letterhead. Yes, the Talone family would want to know and remember this castle-building side of sweet Julie, and knowing it would make them proud.

I found the letterhead among my scraps of notes and laid it on the lectern. Julie had summarized her highest aspirations in the lines of a short poem. Then I heard my voice saying words, felt my lips shaping the phrases that reported Julie's short-lived odyssey:

> To know yourself, search for truth,
> Nurture justice,
> Know compassion,
> But above all,
> Walk with honor
> And wear the garments of understanding.

"Those were Julie's words," I told her mourners. "This was her quest. In her life, she sought to solve many mysteries, and in her death she taught us a greater sense of its profundity.

"Tagore, writing in *Stray Birds*, says, 'Death belongs to life as birth does. The walk is in the raising of the foot as in the laying of it down.'

"Since the beginning of time, people have struggled with the complexities of life, with its mysteries, with its frustrations, and injustices, with the ambiguity of 'to be or not to be." Since the beginning of time, many cultures have chosen not to speak of self-destruction, to shroud it in silence, and to deny it. And because we as a people so often deny death as a part of life, it has enormous power in our lives.

"I believe with all my heart that those things we can bring to light and deal with will lose their destructiveness, and those things which we deny, claim power which is destructive. We must learn that death gives meaning to life so that we can value today and now and each other.

"And so it is that the Talones have asked me to speak today and to share some thoughts with you so that we shall not deny, so that we face reality and pain, and so that we face each other openly and hide nothing.

"Three years ago, my son made a choice to end his life. My family has survived and so can the Talones. We did it by recognizing that there's a time to be sad and a time to cry, and a time to love each other. These are all part of healing.

"I want to share with you part of a letter written to me by a special friend of my son's which deals with the unanswerable 'why' of suicide. It was a comfort to me and hopefully it will be to you.

"This friend wrote: 'His cry was a complex one. For some people, it is not enough to follow the easiest path. When one absorbs so much of the world as Mitch did, there is a need to express it. This is not easily done. So begins one's search for a place, the time, and the people with whom and where this frustration can be freed. Mitch died in his search. I am happy in the belief that much good will come of his cry. And I am comforted to know that there are those who are willing to aid in our search. For myself, I feel compelled to strive twice as hard to answer what I can in this life for us both. I shall carry him with me always, as within him there is also a part of me.'

"To have been with some of you," I added, "and with the Talones these last two days has been a privilege, an honor, and a gift to me. Our worlds have touched and we are blessed because of that touching. I am truly indebted to the Talones for admitting me into their lives at this time.

"And to those of you who love and support this family, I would say—Build no shrines to Julie, but rather replace your grieving after a time with good memories of her. Speak freely of her to her family and friends and share your remembrances. To speak not of her tends to deny her existence. To speak freely tends to affirm her life.

"Be open to your healing. Let it begin with love from each other. This takes time. Free yourself from denying, from bargaining, and from guilt and anger by experiencing these emotions, so that you can one day get beyond this day.

"We can make meaning out of the meaninglessness of Julie's death by recommitting our lives to unconditional love of each other every day of our lives. I believe in an all-loving God who is with us in our pain. I do not believe that God brings tragedy upon us, but I know he is available to love and support us when it strikes.

"We cannot control what happens to us, but we can take charge of how we respond. We can choose to survive or we can choose to be devastated. I can no longer influence the destiny of my own loved one, but I can make certain that my life will become more meaningful as a result of my experience with his chosen exit.

"Yes, we *can* survive. Albert Camus said it so beautifully: 'In the midst of winter,' he wrote, 'I finally learned that there was in me an invincible summer.'

"My 92-year-old aunt wrote about her own vision of hope in these words:

> These days are the winter of the soul,
> but spring comes and brings new life
> and beauty because of the growth of
> roots in the dark. . . .

I repeated the last phrase softly: "Spring comes . . . because of the growth of roots in the dark. . . ."

Suddenly, I felt empty. But at the same instant I felt buoyant and renewed as if wings were attaching themselves to Julie's words, and to Camus', and to my aunt's, and to some of my own. My chair, when I reached it, was like a warm beach gained after a hard swim.

The precise routine of the service continued briefly. The casket was wheeled to the hearse, the family was helped to a limousine, the guests were moved gently toward the exits. Now, only one act of our tragedy remained unplayed. I joined the other actors in the slow procession to the cemetery.

19
My Son...My Son...

The view from within the gate, after one enters the cemetery grounds, is expansive and reassuring. This uncluttered section was without tombstones. As far as the eye could see, parklike slopes tilted gently toward a shining lake. As we drove to the far end where Julie's body would lie, I saw the outlines of hundreds of bronze tablets inlaid in flat granite slabs.

Julie's grave lay half-a-hundred yards up a hill, overlooking acres of maple and oak trees, Georgia pines, and rippling water. A green, canvas canopy on stainless steel legs surmounted her burial place.

Many mourners had arrived and were clumped across the hillside. Others were parking their cars or climbing the slope. As I joined the climbers, carefully dodging the rows of grave markers, I saw a bedraggled bundle of faded blossoms lying almost in the shadow of Julie's canopy. Some earlier mourners had probably left it there in memory of a treasured life. Ahead, I saw piles of fresh blooms still glistening with greenhouse moisture flanking Julie's coffin. The contrast created a twinge of sadness and I bent quickly, hoping that no one was noticing, and lifted the lifeless bouquet from our path and deposited it safely behind a tree.

Pallbearers had already carried the coffin from the hearse to the grave and locked it into the embrace of a mechanical elevator that would, at the pressing of a button, lower its burden. Cathy and her daughter, Cindy, Bill and their two sons, plus a handful of relatives, sat on folding metal chairs. The funeral director flung out a long, white hand and the signal brought the Unitarian minister to a position between the coffin and the assembled mourners. I heard him speak in a voice as cool and soft as freshly-shoveled earth.

The graveside service of a modern funeral is sanitized and mechanized. Further up the slope a small bulldozer waited, ignition off, for the signal that would bring it down the hill to push dirt onto Julie's casket. To one side, apart from everyone else, a cleanup crew wearing soiled Levis and bored expressions lolled in a shady spot awaiting their cue. Under their ministrations, given thirty minutes, the earth's wound would be closed and bandaged with blossoms and no one would know, unless they saw her name inscribed in bronze or unless they remembered that Julie had ever lived.

The minister's voice mingled with birdsong and stifled sobs. My thoughts drifted to my last three days and nights and to the telephone conversation with Cathy when she had accepted my offer of help. Unstintingly, she and her family had given me their trust. In turn, I had emptied myself of every method of survival I had learned during my own bitter years. By now the common-sense injunctions that enabled me to endure had become instinctive. Positive thoughts had replaced negative despair. My good friend's prophecy of years ago had come true: There had been a gift concealed in my son's suicide, many gifts, and reality had inclined me toward an infinitely rewarding journey.

My earnest words—my life, too, I hoped—had persuaded the Talones that all their future happiness depended on their resurrecting memories of Julie, their openness to grief, and their working through the stages of anger and guilt. Tradition would fight them at every turn, I had emphasized. Outdated custom would urge them to wear black, accept the role of being mortally wounded, submit to coddling and protection, and always surrender to the pressure of "what will people think?"

A funeral, I had also learned, could be either a calming or destructive energizer of latent anxiety and fear. I found myself praying that this family would emerge from this valley of death with worthwhile memories of Julie and with peace of mind.

Almost before I was aware of it, mourners about me were standing on tiptoe, watching the gray coffin as it sank. I heard a valedictory "amen," followed by the hum of many voices. Friends began to move forward to speak to the family. The bored workmen got stiffly to their feet. Fifteen-year-old Cindy rose hurriedly from her metal chair, walked to the open grave, and bent low over it as if searching for her lost sister. Well, it's over, I thought, turning away.

My skin suddenly prickled at a shuddery, drawn-out cry. Once in the past I had heard that same, broken-bodied wail from myself, but now it came from Cindy. She was standing above the vanished coffin, pointing down, her body forming an arc of frozen distress, saying hoarsely, "It's backwards . . . it's backwards."

What's backwards? I wondered as I hurried to her. Someone was saying, "It makes no difference, Cindy. It's over. Julie is gone. It doesn't matter."

"It does so make a difference," Cindy moaned. "The coffin's put in backwards. Julie was supposed to see the lake."

I knew what she meant. The family had been comforted when they chose this plot by the thought that Julie's body would be facing out over the emerald valley with its bejeweled lake.

The funeral director appeared at my elbow. "What shall we do?" Cindy's voice rose higher, "Turn Julie around. Please turn her around!"

Bill and Cathy, now standing with a group of friends too far away to hear, were the ones to make this decision. I brought them to Cindy's side, explaining. Bill calmly embraced his daughter. "We'll have it changed," he assured her.

The director said, "This is highly irregular. It will take all of thirty minutes."

"Change it," Bill said.

The director backed away, aghast, then turned and gave an order. A nearby truck started with a roar and vanished over the hilltop. The cleanup crew sat down again. Mourners sought shady spots and indulged in small talk. Cindy stood at the grave's edge like a sentinel. I hoped she would always remember that moment, always remember that she had not worried what people would think, but had asked for what she desperately needed in a critical moment.

To be sure, the situation was unprecedented, but it was not a disaster. On the contrary, people were chatting warmly, greeting each other, gesturing, smiling. The scene could have been outside the doors of a church following a good sermon with pastor and parishioners alike relaxing in each other's company under a benevolent sun. All except Cindy. Separated from the others, her eyes fixed on the hilltop where the truck had gone, she waited.

An errant thunderhead crept closer to the sun, dropping a pall over the hillside. A springtime wind squall tossed nearby treetops with sudden violence and made a pennon of Cindy's hair. Then all became quiet. A few people drifted back to their cars. I retrieved the nosegay of faded blossoms from behind the tree where I had left it and returned it to its proper site.

The truck came back loaded with workmen and an array of rods and straps. They lifted Julie's coffin, reversed it, and gently settled it again within its mother clay. This time the alignment was perfect. Now Julie could "see." A wind puff lifted dust and grass about the green canopy and resettled it. Overhead the clouds dissolved and our hillside turned to gold.

As I watched Cathy and Cindy, I rejoiced at their new purposefulness as they selected a handful of flowers from the floral memorials beside Julie's grave. Turning, they came toward me across the shining grass.

"They told us your son's grave is near here. We'd like to go there now if that's okay with you. Will you take us?" Cathy asked, handing me some of their flowers.

We followed the winding road that I had mounted painfully three years earlier. Cindy, Cathy, and I led the way without speaking. Bill and his sons followed. Soon, we were alone at the high place that sheltered my son's remains. My heart was beating faster than usual, but the ache of intolerable grief was gone. Instead, I felt a sense of sadness and regret but also a profound feeling of appreciation for my child's life.

At his graveside, Cathy knelt and placed a tiny bouquet atop its nameplate. Daughter Cindy followed her lead with head bowed, her shoulders quivering. Obviously she was still carrying a painful burden. As we walked away, I wondered if my misted eyes had really seen that the flowers they left were really buds, symbolizing new life and hope.

At the driveway, we all embraced and then they got into their car and drove away. My last sight, as I strained to catch a glimpse that might indicate the course of this day's struggle, was the stained, tear-streaked face of Cindy. She was holding up a hand and waving.

Alone finally, I returned to "my" grave. My hands had carefully cradled the spray of flowers the Talones had given me. A flash of torment turned my mind backward briefly to that day many months earlier when I had stood in this same spot and railed at God like a fishwife. Now it was my turn to rejoice.

My fingers opened, spilling my blossoms across the letters below, across my child's birthday and deathday.

"My beloved son," I said. "My dearly beloved son, I thank you for your caring, and for your life."

And then my own tears came, nor did I try to stop them.

20
Living, Loving, and Letting Go

Since Julie's death, my contact with the Talones has been limited. Their own struggle to stabilize their lives has been continuous and positive.

Cathy and Bill have attended Atlanta meetings of The Compassionate Friends, a national, self-help organization for parents who have lost children. There they found a support group of understanding fellow-mourners who survive the grief process together through mutual tears and laughter, sharing and comfort. Cathy and Bill are working, traveling, and rebuilding their lives.

Sam, the oldest son, is continuing his college education; Cindy has a job and a steady beau; and Matt, now 14, is coping with the temptations and pressures of adolescence.

I think the Talones would agree that their first year after Julie's death was the hardest—the first Christmas, the first birthday, the first anniversary of her death, all difficult times full of sadness and longing, milestones to be lived through so that one day they may discover that their lives can be more meaningful than ever before. My experience with the Talones, a treasured gift, shall always be a part of me, remembered with love and gratitude.

Perhaps as they search for their gift hidden in Julie's death-by-suicide they will one day agree with Helen Keller's words:

> What we have once enjoyed
> we can never lose.
> All that we love deeply
> becomes a part of us.

21
L'Envoi: The Summing Up

The telling and sharing of the stories of Julie and my son have been a part of my healing. The stories are unique as is the experience of all those who mourn. One develops his own process, I find, and makes his own way in his own time. My hope is that I might add a dimension to the healing of others through affirmation of themselves and their own process, or through renewed hope of survival.

There are no perfect formulas for living through the loss of a loved one who has completed suicide. There are no absolutes, no real guidelines, only the sharing of common experiences and reactions that occur.

No words can explain adequately the phenomenon of self-destruction. Nor can spoken language instruct a family in how to survive. As yet, we know no final answers. Hence, we must be satisfied with partial explanations, with guesses, and with the knowledge that each incident is different. True, there are common denominators but ultimately we must search for our own piece of the truth by living through the questions.

When you are searching for truth, Richard Felder, M.D., of Atlanta, recommends that: "Whatever you can find out about your feelings, or find inside yourself about the suicide, is the only way you can ever be real about it. Face it, whatever it is."

What is certain is that death is a life event, a life change, a rite of passage. It elicits powerful feelings from deep levels within ourselves, feelings not usually evident in day-to-day living. A suicide in the family may magnify these feelings and impose a heavy burden on those left behind. The deed may involve more than the destruction of the person who pulls a trigger or swallows an overdose. Too often, it destroys others in the family, devastating them with the stigma of suicide, of personal guilt, plus the shattering of lifetime relationships. A father whose 16-year-old daughter took her own life says, "Suicide is not a solitary act. A beloved person thinks he or she is killing only herself but she also kills a part of us."

A national, self-help group called Compassionate Friends recently held its fifth annual conference in Chicago. Sascha Wagner, therapist and mother of a girl who took her own life, told an audience composed of surviving parents: "Some of us get desperate and don't make it through. Others of us manage to make it, and there's a specialness about such persons. . . . They have an inheritance, and they kind of become a living memorial to their dead children. Those who survive—that's us—they make the difference that keeps the trees growing."

Much has been written about the stages of grief. I prefer to summarize the impact of grief as I have experienced it, and to share what many people typically go through. I remember the words of Jeff, a young man whose mother had died a year earlier. "You build your own grief process and you build your own recovery," he said. "It's not right or wrong, good or bad. It just *is*."

The impact of suicide is felt emotionally, physically, intellectually, and spiritually.

Emotional trauma includes painful feelings, fears, and longing for the absent one.

Physical reactions include aching, crying, upset stomach, inability to sleep, loss of appetite. They also include one's search for the physical presence of the deceased, and the painful regret that one will never touch or feel that person again.

The intellectual response asks how, when, where and especially why. One struggles in vain to understand what has happened and to make rational sense out of it.

The spiritual response is difficult to capture in words. Certainly, it seems true that a suicide seems to batter one's soul so violently that it is altered forever. At first, one feels utter emptiness, a void, as if the spirit has died. In time, this sensation somehow seems to connect us to universal truth, to the mystery of life and death, and to the collectiveness of mankind. As thoughts and feelings cascade through one's nervous system, the mind surprisingly becomes acutely aware of the far-flung universe and finally of our own impermanance.

Sasha Wagner explains, "It elicits courage from us and calls us to do a greater thing with our lives. Profound grief somehow makes one more honest. If you succeed in working it through, you end up by knowing who you are. It produces wonderfully spiritual feelings. You will know in your solar plexus that it is part of the truth."

The impact of suicide usually begins with a shock, and with disbelief. The questions of how, when and where are immediately asked. Accurate information usually is not available as one tries to understand what has happened. Finally, when the truth sinks in, the mind pleads for an answer to "Why?" What a mystery is encompassed by that tiny word. You will repeat it again and again, sometimes for months, often for years, until finally you understand enough of the truth to go on living.

Most people move unconsciously from the "why" question to "What do I do now?" A small minority may even declare, "I no longer care what happens!" Regardless, whatever happens next is blinding, maddening, and paralyzing for almost everyone.

I shall try to describe my personal tidal wave.

I felt confused, shocked, bewildered, and dazed.

I felt guilty and somehow responsible. "It must be my fault," I said. "I've failed. I must be bad."

I felt personally rejected, which leads to self-pity. "He preferred death to living with me" is one way of putting it. Your rejection leads to the query, "Why me, God? What have I done to deserve this?"

I felt rage, violent and consuming. I was angry at God, then at myself, and eventually at my son. Sometimes, I even felt guilty because I was so angry. A sense of inescapable injustice haunted me.

I felt embarrassment. I asked myself, "What must my friends think of me and of our family? How can I ever face them again? It is so humiliating."

I felt isolated, even though people were all about. It was so easy to say, "Nobody loved him the way I did. No one even understands my pain or sympathizes with it. Worst of all, nobody wants to talk to me about what happened. They all avoid the subject."

I felt helpless, weak, and lifeless. "I can't change my child's death," I thought. "I can't start my life over, and I can't cope."

I felt hopeless, depressed, and suicidal. Like this pain goes deeper and deeper. I can't go on. I want to die."

I felt a sense of relief for whatever reason. I would say, "At least he is no longer suffering as much as he did.

I admit that I felt all those things from time to time but I have talked to other parents who experienced only some of them. But almost everyone experiences fear. Fear is the Mount Vesuvius of emotions. It can rise up from nowhere and turn into a raging volcano. It happens by day and by night and always when you least expect it. In its train are perhaps the cruelest and most poisonous thoughts known to man. Such as:

"I'm going crazy. I set the table for him again today which makes at least a half-dozen times. And I can't stop crying. All day long, I keep asking myself if I'm slipping in and out of spells of madness."

"I'm hopeless. I can't make it, can't cope, can't live through this pain, and I know I'll never get myself together again."

"I'm losing control of myself. If I ever let myself express my guilt and anger, I'll explode all over the place. If I do that, everyone will know I'm crazy. All I can do is stuff it down inside me and pretend."

"I can't stop re-living that moment. It's up there in my mind, burning like a red hot coal. My nightmares run on through the whole night."

"They say suicide is inherited. Who is going to kill himself next? It could be me."

"I'm just plain bad . . . contaminated . . . foul; I must be or he'd still be alive. If I've caused one death, maybe I'll cause somebody else to die. I hate myself. I hate going on living."

"I'm told I need help but nobody can help me, not even professionals. They can't understand it if they haven't been through it themselves."

These fragments are only a fraction of the parade of thoughts which follow in the wake of fear. Such disintegration is not inevitable. The destructive burden can be lifted and one's desperation can be turned from the agony of mourning to the wonder of survival. Some of the essential factors are discussed in a chapter I wrote recently for a volume being published as part of *The Family Therapy Collection*. My contribution is called, *"Coping With Suicide."* I suggested these elements as aids to recovery.

1. Basic self-esteem or feelings of worth. If one's self-esteem is minimal, expect difficulty with recovery, especially around the issue of guilt.

2. Communication skills. These skills include willingness to express your feelings to others. Denying or hiding feelings may lead to isolation and depression.

3. Knowledge of the grief process and your personal history with respect to handling a loss. First, are you acquainted with the conventional steps of the grief process; if not, are you willing to learn them. Second, are there incidents in your own life dealing with loss or death to permit a feeling of hope of surviving?

4. Acceptance of your humanity and your vulnerability. In the past, have you experienced both success and failure, so that you are aware that life encompasses both? If you can answer "yes," that affirmation may determine how guilt is resolved and whether it can be turned into regret through forgiveness of yourself and of others.

5. A good support system. Are you isolated and suffering alone, or do you have one or more friends and peers who are available for sharing and supporting? Is there a nearby grief group or a chapter of Compassionate Friends that you can attend? (see Appendix D).

6. Ability to handle stress and to solve problems. The power of analysis plus a capacity for making decisions speaks well for recovery. You gain strength and courage from handling past experiences.

7. Your spiritual resources and beliefs. Affirmative attitudes

toward God, death, and the meaning of life and afterlife, these are all helpful to one's healing. God's Grace and the Holy Spirit are healing, centering, and empowering to those who believe.

8. A willingness to accept professional help. One of the best reservoirs of experience available to survivors of suicide lies with professional psychologists, psychiatrists, and counselors. They are available usually through local and regional mental health centers. A sufferer must take the first step (which is finding someone who satisfies your needs) and then be willing to work through the prescribed course of therapy.

9. The willingness to laugh with others and at yourself offers a tremendous healing potential.

So how did I survive?

I survived by looking inside myself for truth, by connecting to family and friends, and by ultimately choosing to survive.

I accepted professional counseling to help me express my intense feelings of guilt and anger, and to support me through the process of mourning. I struggled with the question of "why" until I satisfied myself that I could live with partial answers. To go on living, I finally realized, I didn't *need* to know Mitch's reasons.

I gave myself time to heal, which takes a lot longer than the world imagines. Sometimes a couple of years are needed before closure of grief is achieved. Some people I know postpone the pain of the working-through process by denying (in their private minds) that a suicide happened, and they doggedly affirm this denial until months or years have passed. Whatever time it takes is the time it takes and you cannot rush it.

Postponement however, introduces a danger. For some persons, grief and mourning may become a way of life. Drawn-out grieving seems to be their way of seeking nurture and getting attention. Or it can be a sign of self-punishment. If it threatens, professional counseling is helpful and might even be life-saving.

It was Rev. Al Widener, a pastor in Atlanta, well-known for his compassion and for his grief counseling, who first asked me to co-lead a support group for bereaved parents. More recently, I organized a similar group exclusively for persons who had survived the *suicide* of a loved one. Young people, parents, and grandparents attended. The benefits of our discussions have been remarkable. Through sharing our common experiences, we have learned that we are not alone in feeling baffling emotions, and that there is hope for surviving the nightmare.

From time to time, I have asked these survivors to tell me the ways the support group has helped. Here are some comments:

"It is so reassuring to learn that others have lived through the same thing."

"When I hear people saying that life is difficult and unfair, I know my own anger is a common experience. If I can accept that, it helps."

"I am glad to be told that there is no right or wrong way to grieve, because we all grieve differently."

"Talking with others helps me to give myself permission to feel whatever I feel and to say whatever I have to say."

"I've learned to ask for what I need."

"I've learned to give myself time to heal."

"Being reminded that I cannot persuade anyone to feel bad or to kill himself. Only he can do that to himself."

"Knowing the stages of grief gives me mileposts to measure my progress."

"It's a relief to hear others say that things are not always going to be this bad."

"Looking at the harsh truth helped me most. A suicide is a suicide and I must admit it because I can't live with a lie."

"Trying to remember the good times has helped."

"A wound hurts for a while and then it heals and leaves a scar. To me, that means that I may be scarred but I can still be healed and find joy and meaning in my life."

"I no longer seek just to survive. I want to do a larger thing with my life."

"If other ordinary people have survived this, so can I. And if I can survive this, I can survive anything."

"I've learned suicide is not inherited. It doesn't need to happen ever again in our family."

"To know that it's normal to think about myself dying. I'm not crazy and I don't really have to end my life. It helps to know that such a feeling will usually pass.

"I swim 20 laps a day. I hit the water hard."

"Accepting it doesn't mean I have to like it."

"I've turned guilt into appropriate, well-directed regret."

"I want to understand that his life was not manageable."

"It's a bigger tribute to Robby that I can feel the joy of his life now."

All together, those words encompass the essence of healing. To me, they are special words uttered by special people whose lives are becoming whole again. Our group comes together regularly to talk, to heal, to tell our stories, to remember, and to listen—oh, how we listen—to each other even though the rest of our world has finished listening.

J. Eugene Bridges, Th.M., a psychotherapist at Atlanta's Counseling Center called The Link, recently summarized his work with families in the aftermath of suicide. "First encourage them to know it's all right to sit down and remember their life with the person. In this way the family member or members who have come for counseling are helping to bring order into their lives, and—in a mystical way—helping to bring order out of the chaos which erupted with the suicide. The sitting down is the beginning. Second, is the remembering. And with remembering, acceptance begins to set in and, after a while, the people are ready to adjust and to get up and to move on. My belief is that in therapy they sit down and remember and that will enact the healing process and the grief process which have been tragically disengaged by the person's choosing to take his life into his own hands."

Moving on does not mean forgetting. It means gaining a freedom through the opportunity of closure. It means giving up being a victim. It means having the compassion and the courage to say, I don't like being miserable. It means getting on with our lives, with relationships, with work and play, with living and growing.

One more vital step must be discussed. I call it *commitment*. Nancy Hogan, RN, MA, writes of the importance of "a commitment to the memory of the deceased and a commitment to the survival of the family." She argues that these two affirmations are essential "for a positive resolution of the crisis." I heartily agree.

"Whether the suicide is completed by a child, a parent, a spouse, or a sibling," she says, "the family system will be in a crisis state as all of the pieces that fit together to make it a special family become disorganized and are then reorganized into a new, small family. Family members need to be assured that the disorganization that occurs with tragedy is normal and in time the family will have understandable rhythms again."

My family and I went through it all, painfully but precisely as she says. We didn't expect it, didn't want it, and were not prepared to handle it effectively. Abruptly, our lives were irrevocably changed. And our family became smaller by one beloved unit. But presently it would grow, as families do, by the marriage of our oldest son John, now 28, to Cathy Dillon, and by the birth of their two daughters, Amy and Kimberly.

Earlier, I mentioned the importance of friends and peers in the healing process. In this, we have been fortunate. For instance, Bill Sunderland, a talented friend and artist, carved a piece of stone into a sensitive work of art in memory of Mitch. It stands in our front hall as a joyous tribute to his life and to the friendships which sustain us. Others have joined our family group from time to time and, through their love and compassion, brought to us many opportunities for loving and sharing.

Indeed, we found it a pleasure and a necessity to make a commitment to survival, *and also to much more.* Mere survival is restrictive; oftentimes it is selfish. Over recent years, our commitment has become our way of life. I wish I could explain how it works. For one thing, we all value each other more. We appreciate the other fellow's needs, his tastes, and his differences. We respect time and space in a new way, acknowledging daily our new awareness that life is tenuous and a precious treasure. To some extent, we have learned to respond affirmatively to problems, to a crisis, and even to chaos.

Don't misunderstand me. We are not always efficient or perfect. Nor do we always do well or wisely. Yet, despite our blunders, failures, and mistakes, we manage to cope. And to cope—with love. There! I've said it. To cope with *love.* Surely that is the secret balm that holds the human family together. With such a plan, we know we are not helpless.

And we remember our star-crossed son and brother, Mitch. Especially we remember him on such occasions as the anniversary of his death, his birthday, and at Thanksgiving or Christmas. Last year, we honored his death-day by going out to dinner as a family. At the table, I proposed a toast. Holding up my glass, I looked around and said, "To Mitch."

Twenty-year-old Bob was startled. "To Mitch?" he questioned.

"Yes," I replied. "To his *life* and to the good times."

Smiling, he said, "Yes, here's to his *life.*"

Several years after Mitch's death, we found ourselves moving from the house we had occupied for 21 years. Our crew of movers was augmented by son Bill, 22, who came home from the University of Georgia to help, and son Bob who had been living with us while attending DeKalb College, and by husband Jack and myself.

I was cleaning the room that had been Mitch's bedroom but more recently had become my office-at-home. For some unexplained reason, I had been drawn to that room, had sat on the floor, and was picking bits of paper out of the old rug that had never been replaced. Suddenly, my fingers felt the cold metal of a cartridge, and then of another one. Two unfired bullets lay at my fingertips. In this very room, Mitch had shot himself twice. My mind reeled. Those bullets, I knew, had surely been among those from which Mitch had loaded his two revolvers. I picked them up and placed them on my shaking palm. My heart raced and I began to breathe as if I were finishing a hard race.

At that instant, Bob happened to step into the room and his eyes saw what I held. "What is that?"

"These have to be two of Mitch's bullets." That thought bred another. "At least, *these* didn't kill him," I said.

Bob looked into my eyes. "Mom, bullets didn't kill him. Mitch killed Mitch."

A gust of relief swept over me. He was right, of course. Bullets did not do it. For a moment, I had flashed back to blaming an inanimate object. With all the healing I had achieved, remnants of grief were still floating around in my subconscious. What a comfort it was to have a son who saw the truth so readily and so wisely. Not only did he do so on that day but he and Bill and John, in their matter-of-fact way, have reminded me often that dealing with tragedy head-on can produce growth. I know that my three sons stand taller today, testimony that a brother's death can turn young boys into very wise men.

I recall another day when I was cleaning out a closet and discovered some of Mitch's music. His composition, *Love Your Brother*, lay on top of the pile. I was unprepared for the sight of his vigorous handwriting and his sentimental lyrics. Sinking to the floor, I cried in anguish. Bill heard me and came to my side, knelt, and held me while I sobbed. When my grief had subsided, we talked about Mitch and how we missed him. I shall cherish that moment forever. Yet, I almost turned away from him. The impulse came when I first felt his arms around me. I had been reared to be strong. Almost, almost, I had started to utter the words that would assert my strength and imply that I was all right and in control. Instead, I released those taut restraints and let the tears come. And out of the wordless communication between us, a golden memory was created.

Thus I learned lesson number 999.

The impact of Mitch's death on John, Bill, and Bob is their own story, and perhaps another chapter some day. I can say here that their survival and their healing has been a part of mine and that of my husband Jack. We have hurt and cried together. We have felt guilty and angry together. We have laughed, shared, and healed together. We have faced the truth. Today, no secrets haunt us. I know that makes a difference.

Eight months ago, we moved into a comfortable home in northeast Atlanta. Bob has his own room and attends a nearby college. Bill's room is ready for weekends and vacations. Another room holds the toys and trundle beds that are suitable for the children of John and Cathy, while father and mother sleep nearby.

After 30 years of marriage, Jack and I are facing our future with a firm sense of who we are. Our marriage has survived the suicide statistics which say that parents of a child who kills himself often divorce each other. We have survived, I believe, because we were determined that our bonds of loving and struggling should not be broken. We had suffered one loss. We didn't want another.

Yes, we did our grieving within our own beings, in the stillness of our private souls, separate and alone. And we healed in our own ways and according to our own timetables. But at the same time, we shared our sorrows and so received the wonderful kind of healing that comes from dividing a burden. Sometimes we did very well, and sometimes we did not do well at all. But we *did it*. Often, it was difficult because we had no energy to give to the other. Having different needs, it became tempting to blame.

Gradually, as we continued to share and talk, our strength returned bearing the gift of laughter, joy, faith in God, and confidence in the future.

Patricia Sun is a lecturer, healer, and teacher from California, whose workshops and audio tapes contributed much to my recovery. It has been said of her, "Patricia helps you to discover who you are. She empowers you to see more of yourself and how all of you fits into your children, your job, and your life, She teaches you how to move beyond your fears to discover freedom."

Patricia Sun herself says this: "Every time you feel pain, every time you feel despair, every time you feel loss, every time you feel remorse, every time you feel fear . . . it is always your growing edge."

And so it is. . . .

My son . . . my son . . . your life indeed was a precious gift. Unbelievably so were the lessons I learned from living each day for itself, knowing that there may be no tomorrow, but whatever happens I have this day to love, to value, to be. I must have thought that you were immortal, if I thought of it at all, for I never even considered that you might die. Now, you have taught me to revere life. I see that it is precious and fragile and can vanish in an instant. I now look with "seeing" eyes and "hearing" ears. I'm intent on cherishing the moment. What a treasury of lessons your sacrifice has uncovered. Would that I never forget. And if I do . . . because I am human . . . let my scarred heart remind me gently with pangs of missing you.

And help me to be aware always that it is through suffering that we humans meet one another, knowing no strangers, and that life can regain its meaning through that precious kinship.

The End

APPENDIX A

THE SUICIDE OF MY SON

My son lies cruel and cold today,
    He'll never touch another.
My son lay kind and warm before.
    I know—I am his mother.

His troubled heart, his bleeding soul,
    His tortured body lies,
Yet lived he twenty years today,
    And now he's closed his eyes.

His friends parade in solemn quest,
    Searching the world to find
Some meaning or some purpose
    In his tormented mind.

My anger and my burning rage
    Conflict with loving him.
I pray for inner strength and peace,
    For healing to begin.

I seek to still my soul's unrest,
    To calm the hell within;
Not knowing if or how or when
    Acceptance will begin.

I grieve, I mourn, I agonize
    The moment of his death.
I long to feel the sweetness
    And the warming of his breath.

Consuming swells of tears arise
    From depths I've never known;
The memory of his strong embrace,
    The love he's often shown.

Pictures of him living in
    Our home obsess my mind;

My Son ... My Son ...

Playing, fighting, laughing, crying.
    Would that I were blind!

My son, my son, how came you here?
    What answers did you seek?
Alas, you listened not, my dear.
    Did you not hear me speak?

We searched for help, your Dad and I,
    But you would not be saved.
Till now you rest in solemn peace,
    The triumph that you craved.

I knew your selfish pride, my son;
    Perfection was your goal.
If only you had learned, my love,
    That failure makes you whole.

A gift, I'm told, you've left behind,
    That I must seek and find;
But pain too deep, and missing you
    Have blocked my open mind.

I wonder if the gift you left
    Will ever be revealed;
Or still is locked inside your soul,
    Eternally concealed.

My wish, my hope, my trust must be
    Some treasure you'll bestow,
Like tiny sparrow footsteps
    Upon new-fallen snow.

A gift less seen than heard, my son,
    A gift to banish tears,
Composed of thoughts and harmonies,
    Like music of the spheres.

This gift, already shared with us,
    Is music you composed;
It lifts my heart, my spirit soars,
    Though you lie in repose.

This legacy was yours alone;
   It lightened every load,
And yet you knew not of its worth,
   Nor of the joy it sowed.

Your Steinway pays a tribute as
   It stands there all alone,
Recalling tender harmonies
   You played when you came home.

And now I hear recordings of
   Your voice and of your songs;
This precious gift you've given me,
   Will help me to be strong.

With twisted hearts, my loved ones throng,
   Our agonies entwined;
Your music helps to fill the void—
   Shared comfort there we find.

I ache for other mothers, too,
   Across this land of ours,
Whose troubled sons must all be helped
   Before their new wine sours.

Let's not ask why—no answer comes—
   Instead, let's study how
We can prevent their useless deaths.
   Let mankind do it now.

If pain and torment, wave on wave,
   Will ever leave my soul,
O God, I pray what's left of me,
   Will once again be whole.

                . . . *Iris Bolton*
                February 26, 1977

APPENDIX B

THOUGH WE MEET AS STRANGERS, BY OUR LOVE WE SHALL BE KNOWN

I agree that this is one of the worst things that can happen to you in your life. I know because my twenty-year-old son committed suicide. *You can survive it*, even though you may not think so now. Then you will know your own strength. When you've survived this, you can survive all life's tragedies.

You need to talk to each other about your loss and your pain. Talk about the good times you remember and the not-so-good. Keep talking and don't bottle up. All of your feelings are natural. Know this and believe it. Feelings of guilt and anger may be strong and are to be expected.

You may use this time to bring your family closer together or to tear you apart by blaming. *Nobody* is at fault. You may need to feel guilty for a while to eventually know that you are *not* responsible. Sometimes you have to go *through* a feeling to get *beyond* it. Facing death together can give you an appreciation of each other and of life that you never had before. Allow yourself to just *be* and to *be with each other*. There is no right or wrong to any of it.

There are no set rules to follow. Take the lead from your minister or the person making arrangements, but ask for anything you want or need, even if it seems foolish.

My personal faith is in a loving God who is with us through tragedy. I do not believe he caused it or that he allowed it. It just happened. I believe my healing will come through my faith, my family and friends. If your beliefs do not include the concept of God, your comfort and support may come mainly from family, friends and your own inner strength.

You will ask *why* a million times, and you need to ask the question. You may never know the complete answer of why, but it's important to struggle with the question. Then one day you will be able to let it go and not need to know anymore. Then you will be dealing with how to go on with your own lives. The meaning I have found in my own son's suicide is to realize that life is tenuous for us all, so I have the choice of making every minute count with my family from now on and valuing them and friends and life in a way I never did before.

It may be helpful to face the reality that suicide was an apparent solution to overwhelming problems for a member of your family. If you can talk openly with each other or a counselor about other solutions and alternatives to problem solving, this agony may never again touch your family.

Please allow your friends and family to take care of you. This helps you and helps them, too. You don't have to be strong. In fact, crying is natural and healing and keeps you from bottling up your feelings.

Know and expect guilt and anger to be natural and hard to deal with. It may be important for you to someday get angry at him/her. This was important for me to do, even though, at first, I could not get in touch with my anger at all. I finally gave myself permission to be angry at my son for giving up, for leaving me with such pain, for leaving my life, for not allowing me or others to help him, for his choice about his life, and for his lost future and mine with him. When my anger was expressed, I could then let it go, and the anger lost its destructive power in my life.

I struggled with guilt—what had I done or not done that I should have or should not have? I finally realized that I gave my son my humanness . . . my positives and negatives. What he did with that was his responsibility . . . not mine. I could give him total responsibility for his own actions. I could let the guilt and the anger go. I could experience a sense of relief for the end to his pain and suffering. A sense of peace.

In summary . . . be with each other; keep talking to each other; talk about him or her (positive and negative memories); allow your friends to do things for you; make major decisions together; know you will all grieve differently and respect that; allow yourself to cry and release your feelings . . . and *know you can survive*.

My hope for you is that you will go through the mourning and grieving that is needed for emotional healing, and that you, too, will one day find renewed meaning in your own life and hope for the future.

Though we meet as strangers, by our love we will be known.

Iris Bolton

APPENDIX C
FUNERAL ADDRESS
APRIL, 1980

The Talone family asked Iris Bolton to speak at the funeral of their daughter, Julie, on April 11, 1980. This is a copy of her talk.

> "To know you
> Search for truth
> Nurture justice
> Know compassion
> But, above all,
> Walk with honor
> And wear the garments of understanding."

These were Julie's words. This was her quest. In her life, she sought to solve life's mysteries and, in her death, she taught us a greater sense of its profundity. Tagore, in *Stray Birds*, says, "Death belongs to life as birth does. The walk is in the raising of the foot as in the laying of it down."

Since the beginning of time, people have struggled with the complexities of life, with its mysteries, with its frustrations and injustices, with the ambiguity of to be or not to be. Since the beginning of time, many cultures have chosen not to speak of self-destruction; to shroud it in silence and to deny it. And because we as a people so often deny death as a part of life, it has enormous power in our lives. I believe, with all my heart, that those things we can bring to light and deal with will lose their destructiveness and those things which we deny and speak not of claim power in our lives; often destructive power. We must learn that death gives meaning to life so that we can value today and each other and now.

And so it is that the Talones have asked me to speak today to share with you. So we do not deny, so that we face reality, pain, and each other. Three years ago my son made a choice to end his life. My family and I have survived and so can you. This is a time to be sad and to cry and to love each other.

I would like to share with you part of a letter written to me by a special friend of my son's. As it dealt with the unanswerable "why", it was a comfort to me, and, hopefully, will be to you.

"His cry was a complex one. For some people, it is not enough to follow the easiest path. When one absorbs so much of the world, there is a need to express it. This is not easily done. So begins the search for the place, time, and people with whom and where this frustration can be freed. Mitch died in his search. I am happy in the belief that much good, indeed, will come of his cry. And I am comforted to know that there are people willing to aid in our search. For myself, I feel compelled to strive twice as hard to answer what I can in this life for us both. I shall carry him with me always as with him is a part of me."

It has been my privilege, my honor, and a gift to me to have been with some of you and the Talones these last two days. Our lives have touched and we are blessed because of it. I am indebted to the Talones for allowing me into their lives at this time.

And to those of you who love and support this family, build no shrines but, rather, replace your grieving and your pain, after a time, with good memories of Julie. Speak freely of her to her family and friends and share your remembrances with them. To speak not of her tends to deny her existence; to speak freely of her tends to affirm her life.

Be open to your healing. Let it begin with love from each other. It takes time. Free yourself from denial, bargaining, guilt, and anger by experiencing those emotions, so you too can one day get beyond this day.

We can make meaning out of the meaninglessness of Julie's death by recommitting our lives to unconditional love of each other every day of our lives. I believe in an all loving God who is with us in our pain. I do not believe he is all powerful and brings tragedy upon us, but that he is available to love and support us through life's crises.

We cannot control what happens to us but we can take charge of how we respond. We can choose to survive or we can choose to be devastated. I can no longer change the destiny of my loved one but I can be sure that my life will be more meaningful as a result of this experience. 1 can survive. Albert Camus said so beautifully, "In the midst of winter, I finally learned that there was in me an invincible summer."

Sarah Reeves, my 92-year-old aunt, wrote these words of hope:

"These days are the winter of the soul, but spring comes and brings new life and beauty, because of the growth of roots in the dark ... spring comes and brings new life and beauty, because of the growth of roots in the dark."

SUICIDE INFORMATION RESOURCES

American Association of Suicidology
2459 South Ash Street
Denver, Colorado 80222
Executive Officer: Julie Perlman
(303) 692-0985
For a Directory of Survivors of Suicide Support Groups..(SOS) or information regarding Survivors Newsletter, write AAS above.

American Suicide Foundation
1045 Park Avenue
New York, New York 10028
(212) 410-1111
Executive Director: Dr. Herbert Hendin

The Compassionate Friends, Inc.,
(for bereaved parents)
National Headquarters
P.O. Box 3696
Oak Brook, Illinois 60522-3696
(708) 990-0010

Suicide Information & Education Center
Number 102
723 14th Street N.W.
Calagary, Alberta T2N 2A4 Canada
(403) 283-3031

APPENDIX D
BEYOND SURVIVING

1. Know you can survive. You may not think so, but you can.
2. Struggle with "why" it happened until you no longer need to know "why", or until you are satisfied with partial answers.
3. Know you may feel overwhelmed by the intensity of your feelings but all your feelings are normal.
4. Anger, guilt, confusion, forgetfulness are common responses. You are not crazy, — you are in mourning.
5. Be aware you may feel appropriate anger at the person, at the world, at God, at yourself.
6. You may feel guilty for what you think you did or did not do.
7. Having suicidal thoughts is common. It does not mean that you will act on those thoughts.
8. Remember to take one moment or one day at a time.
9. Find a good listener with whom to share. Call someone.
10. Don't be afraid to cry. Tears are healing.
11. Give yourself time to heal.
12. Remember, the choice was not yours. No one is the sole influence in another's life.
13. Expect setbacks. Don't panic if emotions return like a tidal wave. You may only be experiencing a remanant of grief.
14. Try to put off major decisions.
15. Give yourself permission to get professional help.
16. Be aware of the pain of your family and friends.
17. Be patient with yourself and with others.
18. Set your own limits and learn to say no.
19. Steer clear of people who want to tell you *what* or *how* to feel.
20. Know that there are support groups that can be helpful, such as The Campassionate Friends or Survivors of Suicide Groups. If not, ask a professional to help start one.
21. Call on your personal faith to help you through.
22. It is common to experience physical reactions to your grief, i.e. —headaches, loss of appetite, inability to sleep, etc.
23. The willingness to laugh with others and at yourself is healing.
24. Wear out your questions, anger, guilt, or other feelings until you can let them go.
25. Know that you will never be the same again, but you can survive and go beyond just surviving. . .

THE GRIEF AND THE MOURNING PROCESS

After a death by suicide, there is a need to understand *why*. You need to ask that question, but you may never know the answer. A combination of significant and contradictory factors seems to be present. One result is that a survivor often seems to be hapless, helpless, and hopeless.

HAPLESS! Some people who have self-destructive tendencies also appear to have a helpless quality about their lives. One thing after another goes wrong. Such persons may over-react in a negative way and, as a result, start to feel. . . .

HELPLESS!! - He or she doesn't know how to get back on track. If one's helplessness continues and deepens, that person may become. . . .

HOPELESS!!! - And so the will to live diminishes and disappears.

Other Important Factors

* * * There is a loss of important relationships.
* * * Introspection increases; so does self-criticism.
* * * You feel an internal pressure to achieve and produce, which pressure may be brought on by an environment that encourages perfection and over-achievement, or by school or peer pressures.
* * * The size and mobility of one's family can create complications.
* * * Developing sexuality may complicate matters.
* * * One's mourning may involve a cutting of personal ties which are the source of one's value system, security, and family approval.
* * * Conflicting values between what an adolescent believes and what he sees in the real world produce a situation which causes turmoil, hostility, and disappointment.
* * * Biological changes take place within the body.
* * * The abuse of drugs and alcohol, causing depression and the loss of control over one's life; indeed, hallucinogens themselves can be a direct cause of death.
* * * The mistaken belief that suicide is the only solution, a conclusion reached after all other efforts to cope have failed.

The Phases of Grief

There is no right or wrong way to grieve. All your feelings are normal. It is helpful, however, to know that human grief is a process that often follows a healing pattern.

Shock is the first stage. It is accompanied by disbelief and numbness.

Denial follows quickly, crying "I don't believe it," or "It can't be."

Bargaining is your promise that "I'll be so very good that maybe I can wake up and find that it isn't so. I'll do all the right things if only. . . ."

Guilt is painful and hard to deal with. This is when one says over and over, "If only I had . . ." or "If only I had not . . ." This is a normal feeling and ultimately it may be solved by stating, "I'm a human being and I gave the best and worst of me to my friend and what he or she does with that is his or her responsibility."

Anger. Anger is another big factor which seems to be necessary in order to face the reality of life and then to get beyond it. We must all heal in our own ways. Anger is a natural stage through which we must pass. Your anger at your deceased loved one may even make you feel guilty, or it may be because your own life continues whereas your friend's life is over.

Depression. Depression is a stage of grief that comes and goes. Knowing this, be prepared to give yourself time to heal. Resignation is a late stage. It comes when finally you accept the truth.

Acceptance and hope! Understand that you will never be the same but your life can go on to find meaning and purpose.

WHAT TO DO

Share your feelings with someone.
Discuss those feelings openly and frankly.
Show interest and support to those who need your help
Get Professional Assistance!

SUICIDE IS A PERMANENT SOLUTION TO A TEMPORARY PROBLEM

WHEN A LOVED ONE HAS DIED

Know that everyone handles grief in his own way. Know that each person grieves individually. It helps to keep this in mind. When the death is that of a child, be aware that there will be a depth and range of feelings. It is important to honor and respect the needs of survivors in the following days, weeks, and months. Often, you will feel helpless.

Hereunder is a list of some of the things that may be comforting to survivors, and also a list of some things which may be less than helpful. We call these the DO'S AND DON'TS of bereavement.

Here is our "DO" list:

Do Respond honestly to questions asked by the family. You need not answer more than asked. If they want to know more, they will ask later. Too much information, too soon, can feel hurtful.

Do surround survivors with as much love and understanding as you can.

Give them some private time. Be there but don't smother them.

Show love, not control.

If you make another person dependent on you, both of you may end up in a painful relationship.

Let them talk. Most of the time they just need to hear out loud what is going on in their heads. Usually, they are not wanting advice. Encourage the idea that all decisions are to be made by the family together.

Allow them to decide for themselves what they are ready for. Offer your ideas but let them decide.

Expect that they will become tired easily. Grieving is hard work.

On the occasion of a sudden death, especially in the case of suicide, get the names and phone numbers of everyone at the scene, of everyone who is involved in any way. The family may want to ask questions later. Keep a list of the phone calls you receive, if you are helping in the survivor's home; and of visitors, and of those friends or relatives who bring food or other helpful items.

Keep the mail straight.

Keep track of commercial services, their bills, cards, newspaper queries and notices.

If medications are administered, and you are helping in the home, learn their names and the hours they should be taken.

Offer to help with the documentation required by an insurance company; this usually requires a zeroxed copy of the death certificate.

The insurance agent will tell you what is needed.

If a child has died, pay special attention to that child's brothers and sisters, if any. Do this at the funeral and also during the coming months.

Allow each of them to express as much grief as they are feeling and are willing to share.

Allow them to talk about the special, endearing qualities of the loved one who died.

Here is our "DON'T" list.

Don't assume that you know best.

Don't tell a griever, "I know just how you feel." You don't know!

Don't make comparisons, like saying, "I know how you feel because my own baby (or father or mother or best friend) died and I . . . ." No comparisons, please.

Don't tell them *what* to feel! Let them feel what they are feeling when they are feeling it.

If they are feeling pain or anger and it makes you uncomfortable, don't try to change their feelings.

Never treat them as if they don't have enough sense to make their own decisions, or to understand what they are being told.

Don't preach. If religion is important to them, they will draw strength from it. Don't tell them that what has happened is God's will.

Don't tell them to call you "any time, day or night," unless you are prepared to take a 3:00 a.m. phone call.

Don't ply them with your personal pain-killers such as alcohol, pills or personal medications. Leave that to experts.

Don't repeat over and over your offers to run errands, sweep the driveway, or call mutual friends. Just DO it!

If a child has been lost, don't try to keep a parent from talking about the tragedy.

Don't try to take over. Many mourners wish to remain involved in some activities and responsibilities.

Don't stop seeing them.

No matter who has died, don't let that person's name be tabooed. If he or she is never mentioned, it seems as if everyone wants to forget that such a person once existed. Most families need to hear the name of their loved one over and over.

Don't alter the loved one's room. Do not pick up clothes, or clean the room. When the family members are ready, they will take care of the matter in their own way, or ask for help if it is needed.

Don't let your own sense of helplessness keep you from reaching out to a bereaved person.

Don't try to find something positive (e.g.-a moral lesson, closer family ties, etc) about a loved one's death.

Don't point out, in the case of a child's death, that they have other children. Children are never interchangeable.

Never make a comment which in any way suggests that a victim's care in the home, emergency room, or wherever, was inadequate. Survivors (particularly parents) are plagued by feelings of doubt and guilt, without needing help from their relatives or friends.

ABOUT THE AUTHORS

Iris Bolton is director of The Link Counseling Center, a private, non-profit counseling center in Atlanta, GA. She graduated from Columbia University, attended Georgia State University School in Community Counseling, and holds a master's degree from Emory University. She has received training both here and abroad. She is co-founder of the North Atlanta Chapter of Compassionate Friends, a national, self-help organization for bereaved parents.

She is founder of Survivors of Suicide, an Atlanta support group. She holds memberships in the American Association of Suicidology, the Council for Children, the Mental Health Association of Georgia, and the Governor's Child and Adolescent Services Subcommittee on Mental Health and Mental Retardation. She holds workshops and seminars all over the United States. She is married, a mother (four sons), and a grandmother (two granddaughters). This is her first book.

Curtis Mitchell has written hundreds of articles for leading magazines plus a dozen books. He is also the grandfather of Curtis Mitchell Bolton whose suicide inspired this book.

The Bolton Press, 1325 Belmore Way, NE, Atlanta, GA 30350
Phones: 404-393-1173 - Link Counseling Center 404-256-9797

I understand the price of MY SON...MY SON... is $10.95* plus $2.00 for handling and mailing, a total of $12.95 per copy. My check for ____ copies is enclosed for the sum of $ _____.
(Georgia residents must include 6% Sales Tax on $10.95)

SEND BOOK TO:

Name

Address

City   State   Zip
Phone: (__)_____   Date:_____

*Bookstores, libraries, schools, groups or individuals may order in volume.